ALCATRAZ ESCAPE FILES

FROM THE OFFICIAL RECORDS

GOLDEN GATE NATIONAL PARKS CONSERVANCY
SAN FRANCISCO, CALIFORNIA

Golden Gate National Parks Conservancy
Building 201 Fort Mason
San Francisco, California 94123
www.parksconservancy.org

ISBN 978-1-932519-16-7
Library of Congress Control Number: 2011920110

Unless otherwise indicated below, all documents, inmate mug shots, and photographs are from the Bureau of Prisons files held by the National Archives and Records Administration, San Bruno, California.
www.archives.gov/san-francisco

Golden Gate National Parks Conservancy Collection: p. 164

Golden Gate National Recreation Area/Park Archives and Records Center: pp. iv (background), 4 (lower right), 5, 16, 24, 25, 27, 39, 52, 56, 61, 68, 71, 78, 97, 105, 107 (*Call-Bulletin*), 117–122, 129, 141 (*San Francisco Examiner*), 147 (lower right), 148–149, 151–152, 169, 170, 172

Wayne Padgett: p. 165

San Francisco Public Library/San Francisco History Center: pp. iv (inset), 4 (upper left), 15, 26, 32 (lower right, detail), 38, 138 (lower left), 153

The publisher also acknowledges and thanks Michael Esslinger, author of *Alcatraz: A Definitive History of the Penitentiary Years*, for his generosity and assistance with this project.

Direction: Robert Lieber
Text: Nancy Licht Miljanich
Editor: Susan Tasaki
Design: Alvaro Villanueva
Production: Sarah Lau Levitt, Alan Eckert
Advisors: Michael Esslinger, John Martini
John Moran, Vivian Young

Printed in China

GOLDEN GATE
NATIONAL
PARKS
CONSERVANCY

The Golden Gate National Parks Conservancy is the nonprofit membership organization created to preserve the Golden Gate National Parks, enhance the experiences of park visitors, and build a community dedicated to conserving the parks for the future.

Contents

Keys in prison armory.

Introduction

The inmates' job is to get out; our job is to keep them in.

—USP Alcatraz Correctional Officer

Department of Justice / United States Penitentiary, Alcatraz Island, California / February 1939

PROCEDURE TO BE FOLLOWED IMMEDIATELY ON DISCOVERY OF ESCAPE OR ATTEMPT TO ESCAPE

Immediately upon the receipt in the Armory of advice as to an escape or attempted escape, the siren shall be sounded until ordered to be discontinued. The siren shall be supplemented by a continuous blast of the power house whistle, which also shall be blown until ordered to be discontinued.

All available officers (excepting the boatmen, who shall proceed to the Launch McDowell to await orders) upon hearing these signals shall report at once to the Armory. The first officer reporting to the main office shall be assigned to the officer in charge to assist the officer in the Armory in the notification of the escape . . . and also to assist in the issuance of necessary firearms, and other needed equipment, such as lights for night use.

Upon receipt of needed firearms, all other officers shall be assigned to posts as required by the attending circumstances.

When directed, the Launch McDowell shall immediately start a patrol around the Island, concentrating on the probable places where inmates may seek to enter the waters in the particular escape attempt involved.

It is, of course, understood that all officers assigned to towers or other vital posts shall remain on those posts during the foregoing unless specifically relieved therefrom by the Official in charge.

Every possible aid shall be given Coast Guard, Police or other official agencies assisting in the search. The Chief Clerk's Office, in the event of a successful escape, shall immediately prepare sufficient copies of the prisoner's photograph, descriptive data, and other pertinent information for transmittal at once to the law-enforcement agencies whose services are solicited.

It's two in the morning, and in their cells, the inmates of United States Penitentiary Alcatraz Island sleep as correctional officers make their rounds, counting heads. Then, with a shriek, the escape siren shatters the silence, and the prison goes into lockdown. Outside, searchlights sweep their powerful beams across the rocky terrain and correctional officers scramble for the patrol launch. Another inmate has tried to break the Rock.

On his arrival at USP Alcatraz in 1935, twenty-three-year-old convict Theodore Cole was unimpressed by America's brand-new maximum-security penitentiary. "Don't think I'll like it here," he reportedly boasted. "Doubt I'll stay long." As it turns out, he stayed two years. In December 1937, he and an accomplice made a break for it and were never seen again, either dead or alive. Although officially, no one ever succeeded in escaping from Alcatraz, to this day, Cole and four others are listed in the Bureau of Prisons' records as "missing and presumed drowned."

Escapes, especially successful ones, are the ultimate failure of any prison's security system. In 1933, after selecting Alcatraz Island as the site of its much-discussed "super max" facility, the Bureau of Prisons (BOP) poured approximately $250,000 (in excess of $4 million in current dollars) into making sure escape from the island was impossible. Tool-proof steel bars, multiple guard towers, barbed-wire fencing, tear-gas canisters mounted in the ceilings, gun cages, a tightly guarded armory, the latest in cell-door locking and security devices, a hand-picked and intensively trained custodial staff: in the depths of the Great Depression, no expense was spared to convert Alcatraz from a military prison to America's most secure, most intimidating penal institution. Considering that almost half of the inmates who would be transferred there had a history of

Warden James A. Johnston.

escapes—often successful—from one or more prisons, it was money well-spent.

The first warden, James A. Johnston, had built a reputation for himself at California's Folsom State Prison. Tapped to head the conversion and launching of this new federal institution, he summed up the BOP's mission in a September 1934 interview in the *New York Times*: "Refer to it as a segregation penitentiary. Our new prisoners are not going to know what goes on outside these walls. They will not be permitted to read newspapers or magazines or have visitors. They have been sent here because the government wants to break their contacts with the underworld, and that is going to be done, absolutely."

The BOP's efforts to isolate crime bosses from their network of enforcers and the media created a compelling mystique as far as the public was concerned. In the absence of information about these men and the conditions in which they lived, speculation ran high, and unlikely stories were printed as absolute truth. This mystique also worked to the prison's advantage, however. Because few knew what actually went on there, the threat of being shipped to the island could be used to keep inmates at other prisons in line, or spur them to cooperate. The prospect of being consigned to the Rock loosened tongues and made many a bad guy cringe.

But humans who are locked up can think of only one thing: how to get out. USP Alcatraz inmates played a perpetual game of cat-and-mouse with the correctional officers, looking for weaknesses in the system, moments of inattention, ways to make an end run around the BOP's best-laid plans. During the twenty-nine years Alcatraz was an active federal prison—1934 to 1963—thirty-four men tested its security measures. They were supported by an unknown number of their fellow cons, who helped them secure tools and information or kept a look-out as they sawed through bars or chipped away at openings in the

Warden Edwin Swope.

cell walls. Of the fourteen escape attempts, ten occurred during Warden Johnston's tenure (1934 to 1947). Warden Edwin Swope was more fortunate; no escapes were chalked up during his oversight of the prison (1947 to 1955). Then four more took place, two under Warden Paul Madigan (1955 to 1961) and what turned out to be the final two while Olin Blackwell was in charge (1961 to 1963). With each, both sides learned valuable lessons.

Warden Paul Madigan.

Joseph Bowers, among the earliest prisoners to be transferred to the island, was the first to try to get away; his attempt and his life were cut short by a bullet. In the months following Bowers' death, both guards and convicts processed the lessons taught by this first attempt. The guards learned that threats weren't enough; they had to be ready to use deadly force. The convicts learned that to have a chance at success, they needed more of a plan than just climbing a fence in broad daylight. They also learned that attempting to escape could cost them their lives.

Each year, increasingly accomplished escape artists were sent to this "escape-proof" prison. Of the first group of inmates shipped to the island in 1934, one hundred seventy-eight men had escaped seventy-nine times, attempted escape nineteen times, and been implicated in twelve known escape plots. In the 1935 group, seventy-five had escaped twenty-seven times and had been involved in fifteen escape plots. Housed together, they continued to talk and scheme.

Warden Olin Blackwell.

While no doubt many plans went undiscovered or were foiled by circumstance (or correctional officers' vigilance), fourteen were put into motion. Here are their stories, an account of the men who took on the Rock, drawn from the official records of the Bureau of Prisons, as well as a view from the "other side": a former correctional officer's account of the 1939 attempt (see p. 165).

Escape 1

It Would Take a Madman

Prisoner driven over the edge.

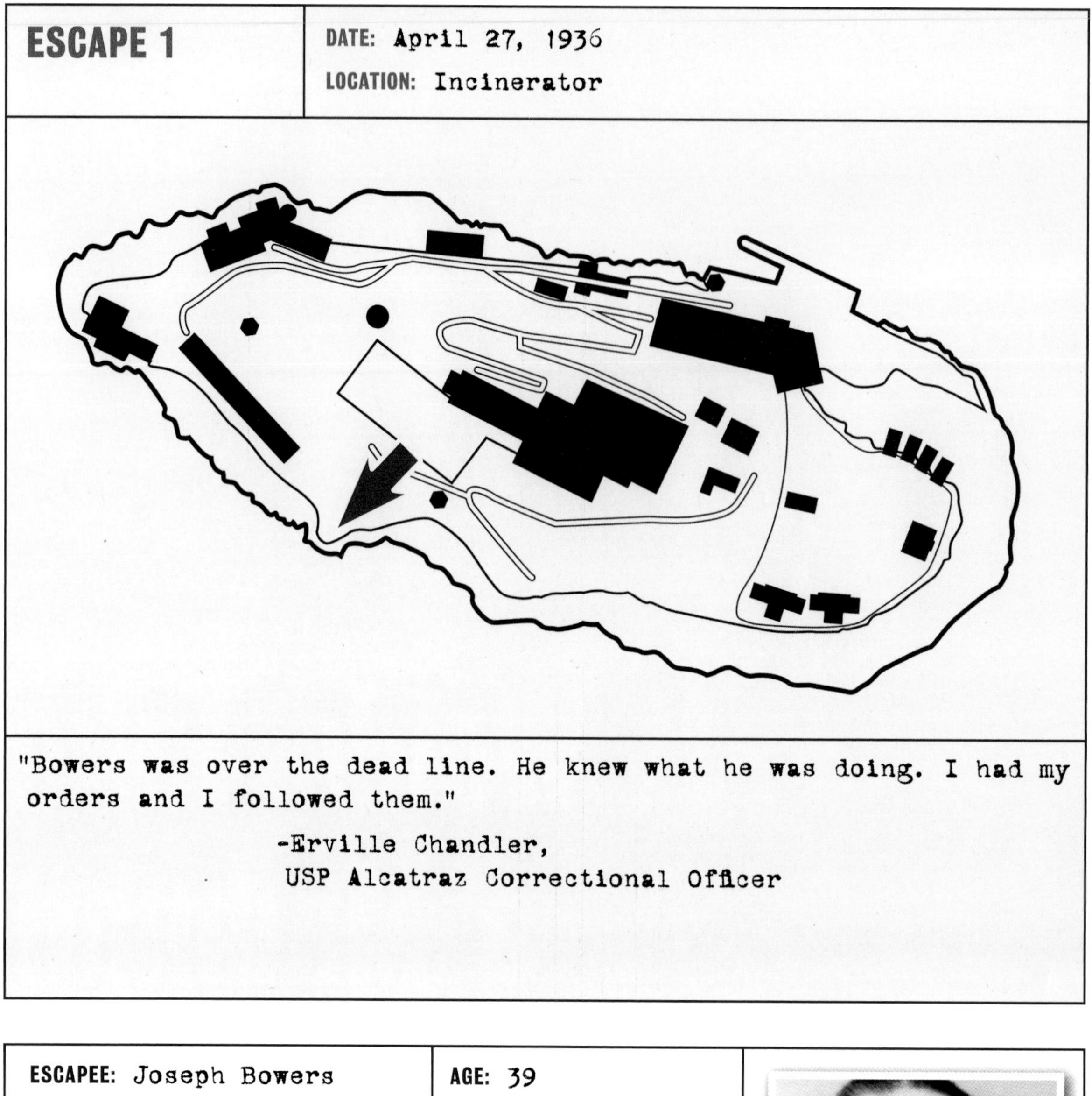

ESCAPE 1

DATE: April 27, 1936

LOCATION: Incinerator

"Bowers was over the dead line. He knew what he was doing. I had my orders and I followed them."

-Erville Chandler,
USP Alcatraz Correctional Officer

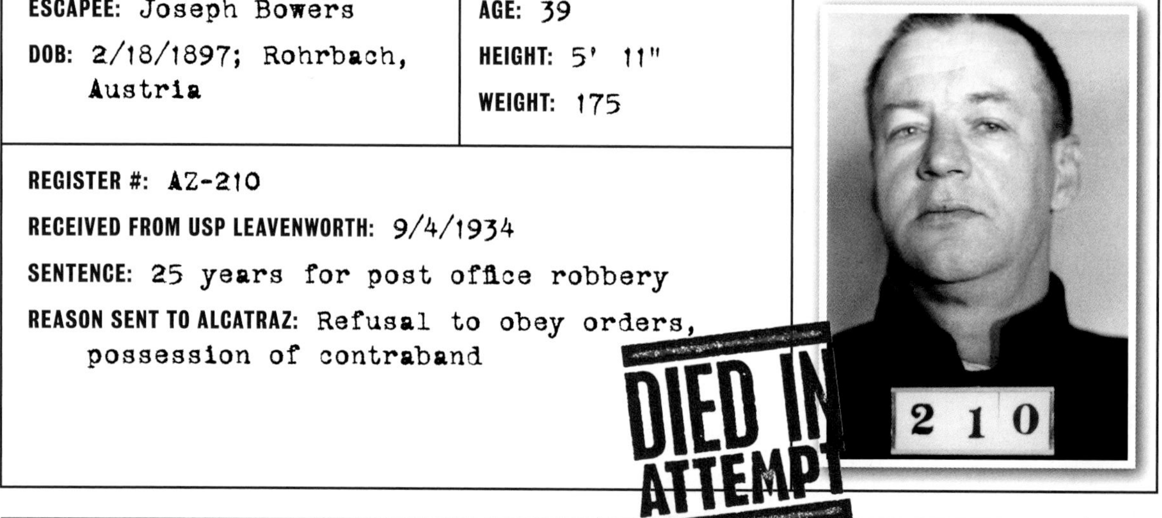

ESCAPEE: Joseph Bowers

DOB: 2/18/1897; Rohrbach, Austria

AGE: 39

HEIGHT: 5' 11"

WEIGHT: 175

REGISTER #: AZ-210

RECEIVED FROM USP LEAVENWORTH: 9/4/1934

SENTENCE: 25 years for post office robbery

REASON SENT TO ALCATRAZ: Refusal to obey orders, possession of contraband

When Alcatraz began operation as America's first federal super-prison in August 1934, it was widely reported to be "escape-proof." Within two years, this claim was put to the test by a man who some of the inmates said was intent on committing suicide and others claimed was the victim of a trigger-happy guard.

Road to Alcatraz

Joseph Bowers' background is murky. At one point, he told authorities that he was born in El Paso, Texas, to circus performers who abandoned him, and had been raised by his parents' circus friends. (In 1933, the German government is believed to have confirmed that he was born in Austria.) At thirteen, he signed on as a merchant seaman and traveled the world. Bowers claimed that he had taken many unusual jobs during his travels, including serving in both the French Foreign Legion and the Russian army. Though he never attended school, he also said he was able to read and write six languages, and had worked as a German interpreter. His colorful list of aliases included Josef Ebner, Ferland Zwonerero, Joe Miller, and Josef Kiehner.

Bowers' encounters with the American criminal justice system began in the late 1920s in the Pacific Northwest. Following his first arrest—for car theft—in October 1928 in Portland, Oregon, he was sentenced to ten months in jail. In November 1930, he was found driving drunk in Vancouver, Washington, and fined $75. Then, on October 2, 1931, Bowers and two other men committed the crime that earned him a federal rap when they robbed a store in Isaiah, California, that also housed a post office. Brandishing weapons, they bound and gagged four hostages, including the postmaster, and got away with $16.63. Bowers was convicted and sent first to United States Penitentiary (USP) McNeil Island and then USP Leavenworth to serve a sentence of twenty-five years.

At McNeil Island, a medical report described Bowers as being in a "constant psychopathic state, inadequate personality, emotionally unstable yet without psychosis." His behavior while incarcerated at Leavenworth, including refusing to obey orders and possessing contraband, led to his transfer to USP Alcatraz in September 1934. At Alcatraz, Bowers continued to violate institutional rules, including the rule of silence (see sidebar, p. 12). His behavior turned violent in March 1935 when he attempted to cut his own throat with a broken eyeglass lens. The report issued following a psychological examination was skeptical of his motives: "The more I listen to Bowers, the less I believe him . . . the recent attempt at suicide has been theatrically planned . . . and resulted in very little damage to him. . . . He is not a normal individual, but he is not so crazy as he is trying to make out."

Nonetheless, Bowers claimed to have epileptic seizures, believed that other inmates were plotting against him, and complained that he could hear voices

9770

CERTIFIED COPY

No. 5400

United States District Court
NORTHERN DISTRICT OF CALIFORNIA
NORTHERN DIVISION

THE UNITED STATES

vs.

Joe Bowers

COMMITMENT
FOR IMPRISONMENT

Rec'd June 25 '32
S. T. Jan. 24, 1949

Offense Postal Laws (Robbery & Assault)
Term 25 yrs. Fine | Com. | Not Com.
Sentence begins March 9, 1932
Parole term October 16, 1940
Short term Jan. 24, 1949
Reports received
Judge's recommendation
District Attorney's recommendation
Date heard and action of board

I, Walter B. Maling, Clerk of the United States District Court for the Northern District of California, do hereby certify the foregoing to be a full, true, and correct copy of the Original Commitment, issued in the case of

The United States vs. Joe Bowers No. 5400

Attest, my hand and the seal of said District Court, this 16th day of June, A. D. 1932.

Walter B. Maling,
Clerk of the U. S. District Court, Northern District of California.

By F M Lampert
Deputy Clerk.

Bowers' prison papers.

Miscellaneous Form
No. 39(b)

SANFORD BATES
Director

DEPARTMENT OF JUSTICE
BUREAU OF PRISONS

WASHINGTON

1747

PER TRANSFER ORDER #________

To the Warden of the U. S. Penitentiary, Leavenworth, Kansas or his duly authorized representative; and to the Warden of the U. S. Penitentiary, Alcatraz Island, California:

WHEREAS, in accordance with the authority contained in Section 7 of the Act approved May 14, 1930 (46 Stat. 325) the Director of the Bureau of Prisons for the Attorney General has ordered the transfer of Joe Bowers #43202 from the U. S. Penitentiary at Leavenworth to the U. S. Penitentiary at Alcatraz Island, California.

NOW THEREFORE, you the Warden of the U. S. Penitentiary at Leavenworth are hereby authorized and directed to execute this order by causing the removal of said prisoner, together with the original writ of commitment and other official papers to the said U. S. Penitentiary at Alcatraz Island and to incur the necessary expense and include it in your regular accounts.

And you, the Warden of the U. S. Penitentiary at Alcatraz Island, are hereby authorized and directed to receive the said prisoner into your custody and him to safely keep until the expiration of his sentence or until he is otherwise discharged according to law.

For the Attorney General

8/15/34 (Date) — Sanford Bates, Director

RETURN OF SERVICE

Pursuant hereunto, I have this 4 day of Sept 1934 executed the above order.

F. G. Zerbst

(Title) Warden

COPY. To be returned to the Bureau of Prisons, Washington, D. C.

talking about him during the night. At his own request, he was frequently admitted to the prison hospital for protection, and was just as quick to demand to be released back into the general population.

Throughout the summer of 1935, Bowers seemed to be in trouble constantly for offenses ranging from talking to attempting to fight a fellow convict and striking an officer. This behavior got him confined to isolation from October 1935 until February 1936. Not long after his release back into the general population, Bowers was put to work at the prison trash incinerator, a job suggested by Warden Johnston, who saw Bowers as "a weak-minded man with a strong back who would get peace of mind by exercising his body." This work detail took place on the island's west side, close to the barbed-wire-topped fence that snaked its way around the island's perimeter.

THE RULE OF SILENCE

In Alcatraz's early days, Warden Johnston instituted rigid controls. One of the most controversial was the rule of silence: prisoners were only allowed to speak when spoken to by staff and could only converse with fellow inmates in the recreation yard and in low voices across dining-hall tables. This rule was a burden to inmates and correctional officers alike, and violations were common. Officer Chandler said the rule of silence "wore on both the convicts and the guards . . . many claimed it drove men mad." After a series of newspaper articles in 1935 and 1936 brought the practice to the public's attention, Warden Johnston ended it in 1937.

The Plan

Was Bowers' escape planned, or a spontaneous act? While it cannot be known for sure, the latter seems like more likely. No tools or other escape-related paraphernalia were found on him and, tellingly, the attempt took place while the director of the Bureau of Prisons, Sanford Bates, was visiting, touring the prison industries shops and meeting with Warden Johnston.

The Escape

Bowers' job assignment was to mash tin cans, burn trash, and send the ash and metal down a small chute into San Francisco Bay. The incinerator stood on a point of land that jutted into the bay, surrounded by a twelve-foot-high

White
3770

white
Vio. P.O. Laws
(Robbery with
firearms)
25 yrs.

UNITED STATES OF AMERICA

In the District Court of the United States

FOR THE NORTHERN DISTRICT OF CALIFORNIA

NORTHERN DIVISION

THE PRESIDENT OF THE UNITED STATES OF AMERICA

To the Marshal of the United States for the Northern District of California, GREETING:

Whereas, at the April 1932 Term of the United States District Court for the Northern District of California, NORTHERN DIVISION, held at the Court Room of said Court in the City of Sacramento, in said District, to wit, on the 16th day of

3202

June, A. D. 1932, Joe Bowers was convicted of the offense of viol. Secs. 197 & 35 CC (1st Ct-assault upon Postmaster having lawful charge of certain mail with intent to rob and putting the life of said Postmaster in jeopardy by use of gun. 2nd Ct- wilfully, with intent to steal, did take away from U.S.Post office for use of defendant personal property of the U.S.

committed on or about the 2nd day of Oct., A. D. 1931, at Isaiah, County of Butte, and within the jurisdiction of said Court, contrary to the form of the statutes of the United States in such case made and provided, and against the peace and dignity of the said United States.

And Whereas, on the 16th day of June, A. D. 1932, being a day in the said term of said Court, said Joe Bowers was, for said offense of which he stood convicted as aforesaid by the judgement of said Court, ordered to be imprisoned for the term of 25 years as to the First Count of Indictment and 10 years as to Second Count of the Indictment. ~~And it was further ordered by the Court that said sentence of imprison~~ment be executed upon the said Joe Bowers by imprisonment in the United States Penitentiary.

Now this is to Command you, the said Marshal, to take and keep and safely deliver the said Joe Bowers into the custody of the Keeper or Warden, or other Officer in charge of said United States Penitentiary forthwith.

And this is to Command you, the said Keeper and Warden and other Officers in charge of the said United States Penitentiary to receive from the United States Marshal of said Northern District of California, the said Joe Bowers convicted and sentenced as aforesaid, and him the said Joe Bowers keep and imprison for the term of twenty-five years as to the First Count of the

of the offense of viol. Secs. 197 & 35 CC (1st Ct-assault upon Postmaster having lawful charge of certain mail with intent to rob and putting the life of said Postmaster in jeopardy by use of gun. 2nd Ct- wilfully, with intent to steal, did take away from U.S.Post office for use of defendant personal property of the U.S.

committed on or about the 2nd day of Oct., A. D. 1931, at Isaiah, County of Butte, and within the jurisdiction of said Court, contrary to the form of the statutes of the United States in such case made and provided, and against the peace and dignity of the said United States.

And Whereas, on the 16th day of June, A. D. 1932, being a day in the said term of said Court, said Joe Bowers was, for said offense of which he stood convicted as aforesaid by the judgement of said Court, ordered to be imprisoned for the term of 25 years as to the First Count of Indictment and 10 years as to Second Count of the Indictment. ~~And it was further ordered by the Court that said sentence of imprisonment~~ be executed upon the said Joe Bowers by imprisonment in the United States Penitentiary.

Now this is to Command you, the said Marshal, to take and keep and safely deliver the said Joe Bowers into the custody of the Keeper or Warden, or other Officer in charge of said United States Penitentiary forthwith.

And this is to Command you, the said Keeper and Warden and other Officers in charge of the said United States Penitentiary to receive from the United States Marshal of said Northern District of California, the said Joe Bowers convicted and sentenced as aforesaid, and him the said Joe Bowers keep and imprison for the term of twenty-five years as to the First Count of the Indictment and ten years as to the Second Count of the Indictment, said terms of imprisonment to run concurrently from March 9, 1932, provided defendant does not appeal or obtain release upon bond.

Herein fail not.

Witness, the Honorable Frank H. Kerrigan Judge of the United States District Court for the Northern District of California, this 16th day of June, A. D. 1932, and of our Independence the 156th.

[SEAL]

Walter B. Maling,
Clerk of said District Court.

By ______________________
Deputy Clerk.

fence topped with three strands of barbed wire. Just beyond the fence, the land dropped away to the island's shoreline fifty feet below. A trained marksman with a high-powered rifle stood sentry about fifty feet away in the Road Guard Tower.

Inmate burning trash.

April 27, 1936, was a typically chilly spring day on the island, with strong ocean winds whipping across the grounds and through the prison. From his work site, Bowers had a 180-degree view of San Francisco and the new Golden Gate Bridge under construction. Ships plied the bay and gulls dipped low overhead as Bowers stoked the fire inside the incinerator's thick cement walls.

Just after 11 AM, the convict work crews were escorted back inside the cellhouse for the noon meal. At that moment, Correctional Officer Erville Chandler glanced down from the guard tower and saw Bowers run toward the fence and begin climbing. Chandler yelled at Bowers to get down, but Bowers kept on. Without hesitation, the trained guard shouldered his Springfield .30 caliber rifle and fired two warning shots, one of which hit the fence and sent metal fragments into Bowers' leg. Undeterred, Bowers continued to scale the barrier.

When gunfire shattered the calm of Alcatraz, Warden Johnston, who was in his office meeting with Director Bates, contacted the armory. Within seconds, the escape siren sounded for the first time on USP Alcatraz, and correctional officers raced to the West Road to assess the situation.

Road guard tower.

Once Bowers reached the top of the fence, he covered the barbed wire with netting taken from the trash and prepared to make his way down the other side. Chandler later said, "If he got to the bay, God knew where he'd go next." The officer drew back his rifle bolt and chambered another round. His third shot hit Bowers in the back near the right shoulder blade and sent him tumbling down to the rocks below.

The Aftermath

The prison launch set out from the dock with armed officers and the prison doctor, George Hess, aboard; Hess pronounced Bowers dead on the spot. Autopsy reports later determined that despite falling more than fifty feet, Bowers' physical trauma was limited to two gunshot wounds, one to his right thigh and another to his upper right chest. A bullet lodged in his lungs caused his death.

Tension ran high between the inmates and the staff for weeks after Bowers' death. Some claimed that Bowers had deliberately committed suicide; others blamed the officer for being too quick to take a kill shot. Correctional Officer Chandler, temporarily reassigned to the prison armory, was ultimately vindicated at the coroner's inquest.

Joseph "Dutch" Bowers was buried at public expense on May 2, 1936, at Mount Olive Cemetery in San Mateo, California. There were no mourners or flowers at his service.

Public fascination with Alcatraz was heightened with the news of Bowers' death. The *San Francisco Examiner* carried an account of the incident in which inmate Henry Young alleged that Bowers had simply climbed the fence to feed a gull. (This report was quickly dismissed, as CO Chandler and other guards at the scene confirmed that Bowers had clearly intended to make his way over the fence.) In a 1938 issue of the *Saturday Evening Post*, a former inmate wrote a sensational piece claiming that during his last year on the Rock, he knew of fourteen convicts who had gone violently insane. While this was not confirmed, it is known that over the prison's twenty-nine-year history, five men committed suicide on Alcatraz.

CORRECTIONAL OFFICER CHANDLER

Erville Freeman Chandler had a long history of distinctive service in the army, navy, and Coast Guard, and won many marksmanship medals. Chandler, his wife, and their young son lived on the island in a parade-ground apartment. Considered by his fellow officers to be "cool-headed and efficient," Chandler was said to have affectionately nicknamed his bolt-action Springfield rifle "Mary-Ann." The investigation after Bowers' death cleared Chandler of any wrongdoing, and he continued his career with the Bureau of Prisons for several more years. His son, Roy Chandler, later chronicled his father's life in *Alcatraz: The Hardest Years.*

Tower guard's "kit."

United States Penitentiary
Alcatraz, California

CONDUCT REPORT

NAME Bowers, Joe. NO. 210.

DATE REPORTED	OFFENSE AND ACTION
Jan.4,1935	REFUSAL TO WORK. This prisoner refused to obey orders. He was told to help with the Laundry downstairs and refused. GUARD I.B.FAULK ACTION: ISOLATION ON RESTR.DIET. & RED.TO THIRD GRADE. C.J.Shuttleworth, Deputy Warden Released from Solitary, Jan 10, 1935 Rel.from Seg. (6 Days) Promoted to second Gr. Apr 4, 1935 Promoted to First Gr. May 4, 1935
June 1,1935	Bowers,while standing in line to be checked out at rear gate kept shouting-"Put me in the dungeon.I do not want to work."C.J.SHUTTLEWORTH,DW. Solitary confinement solid door open,restricted diet.C.J.Shuttleworth, Deputy Warden.
June 20,1935.	Wasting food. Left food in tray after several warnings.GUARD KLEINSCHMIDT. To go without breakfast 6-21-31.C.J.Shuttleworth,Deputy Warden.
July 25,1935	Stalling at Mess.Delaying routine.Is always first one in dining room and has habit of playing with his food until others are through,then delays everyone while he continues to eat. Was warned at breakfast this date but did same thing at noon.Refused to push cup down to end of table when ordered to do so.GUARD R.C.CLINE.To lose supper 7-25-35 and breakfast 7-26-35. C.J.Shuttleworth,Deputy Warden.
Aug.26,1935	Striking an Officer.At mess formation this noon I was talking with Lt. Culver when #210 Bowers,struck me a glsncing blow on the face.There were no provocation of any sort.Lt.Culver and myself grabbed the man securely and placed him in his cell.He was subdued without being struck or harmed. GUARD P.A.HABOUSH.Solitary confinement on restricted diet.E.J.Miller,Act. Depyt Warden. (Out of Solitary Sept 1, 1935 5 days)
Sept.29,1935	Causing confusion in the messhall.This prisoner was talking at the table in Mess Hall,causing confusion.I had to tell him twice before he stopped talking.GUARD I.B.FAULK. To forfeit supper-9-29-35.C.J.Shuttleworth,Deputy Warden.
Oct.1,1935	Wasting food.Left most of his food on his plate at evening meal. (Food inspected by Lt.Culver and found O.K.) GUARD R,C,CLINE. To forfeit breakfast 10-2-35.C.J.Shuttleworth,Deputy Warden.
Oct.26,1935	Creating disturbance & Assaulting an Officer.Creating disturbance in dining room by loud talking and attempting to fight with another inmate,#233-Berlin.While removing this man to Solitary Confinement on Deputy's,orders he rushed at me and struck blindly with his fists.Mr.Lapsley and I overpowered him and placed him in Solitary as directed.GUARDCLINE&HABOUSH.Solitary confinement until futher orders.C.J.Shuttleworth,Deputy Warden.
Jan. 20,1936	Bowers now in Isolation will be fed three meals a day, starting this date. C. J. Shuttleworth Deputy Warden

U.S P.A.C. F. 55

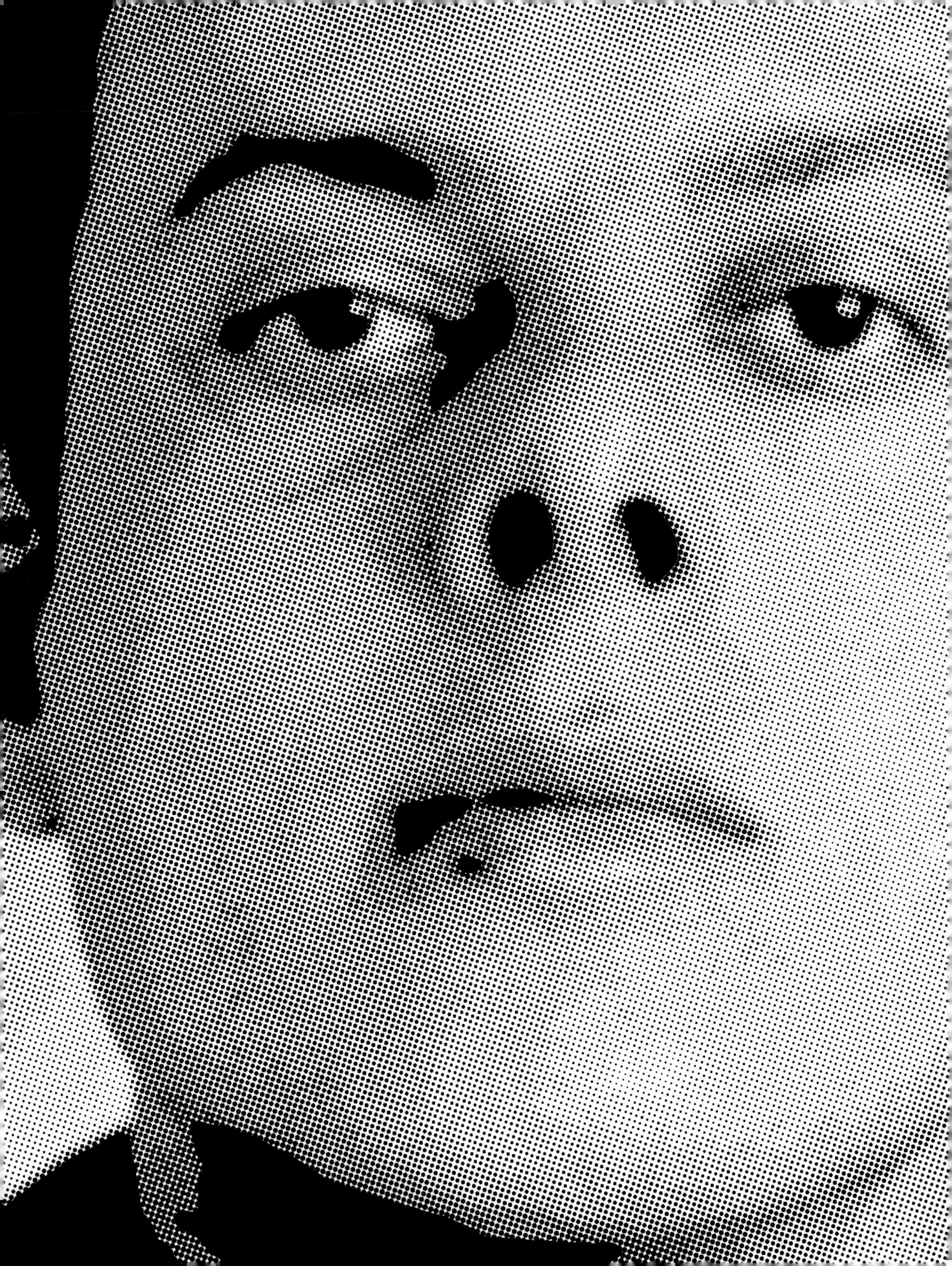

Escape 2

Two Disappear from "Escape Proof" Alcatraz

Prison caught off-guard.

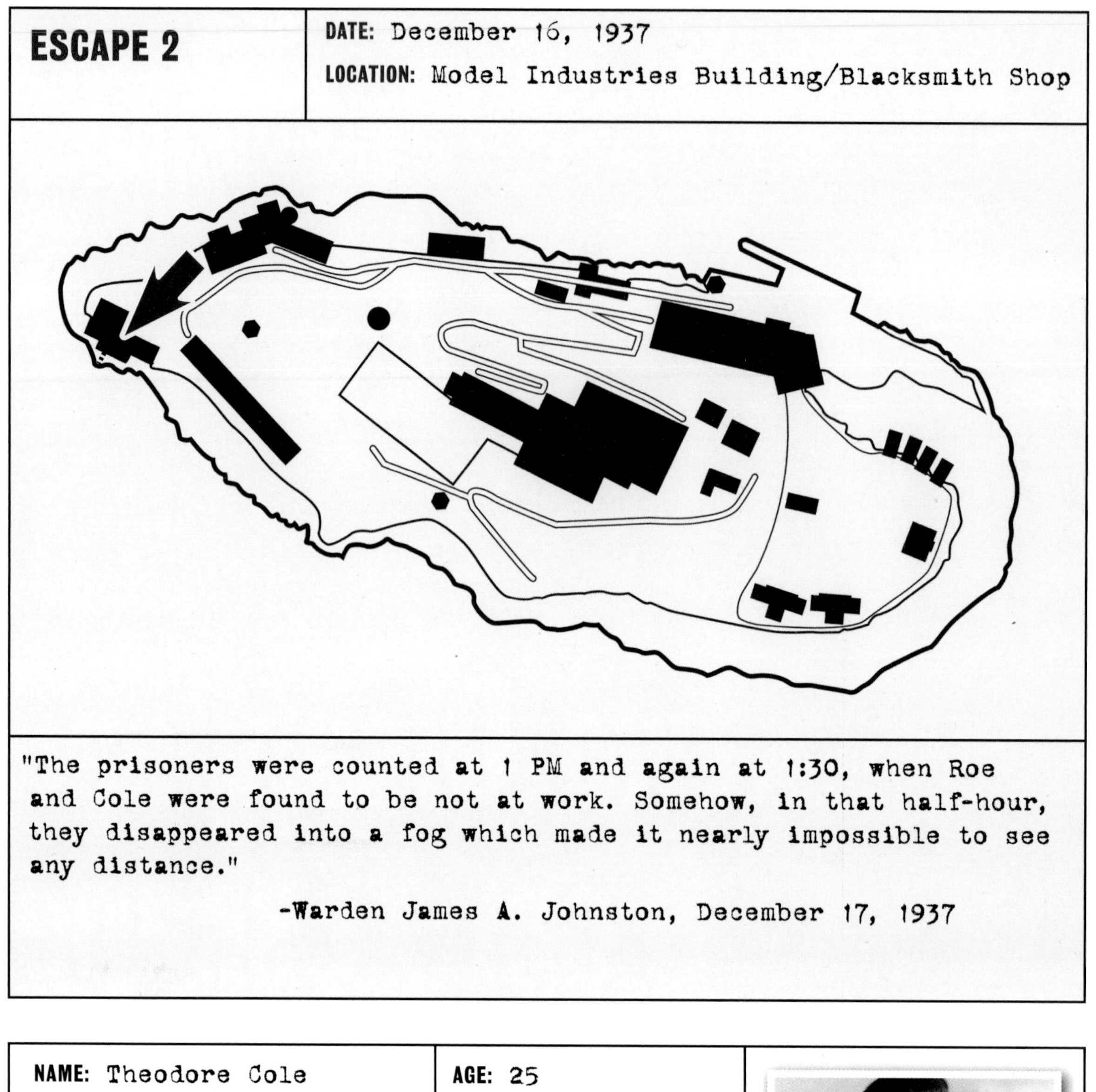

ESCAPE 2

DATE: December 16, 1937

LOCATION: Model Industries Building/Blacksmith Shop

"The prisoners were counted at 1 PM and again at 1:30, when Roe and Cole were found to be not at work. Somehow, in that half-hour, they disappeared into a fog which made it nearly impossible to see any distance."

-Warden James A. Johnston, December 17, 1937

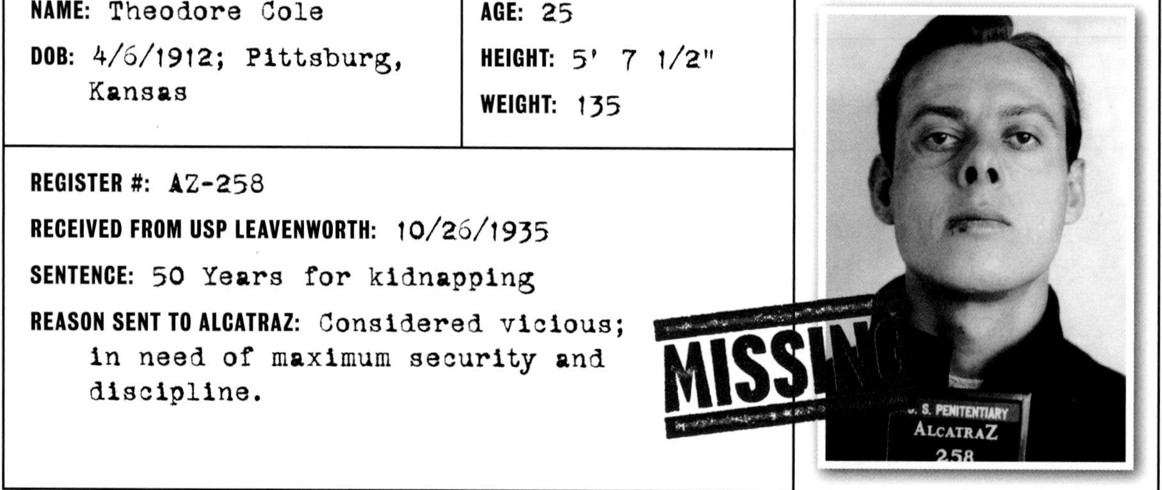

NAME: Theodore Cole

DOB: 4/6/1912; Pittsburg, Kansas

AGE: 25

HEIGHT: 5' 7 1/2"

WEIGHT: 135

REGISTER #: AZ-258

RECEIVED FROM USP LEAVENWORTH: 10/26/1935

SENTENCE: 50 Years for kidnapping

REASON SENT TO ALCATRAZ: Considered vicious; in need of maximum security and discipline.

Both Theodore Cole and Ralph Roe were career criminals with long rap sheets; they also had well-earned reputations as escape artists. Setting off "the most intensive manhunt in recent California history," according to the *New York Times*, Cole and Roe's dramatic escape from Alcatraz was an affront to the government's new maximum-security prison.

Road to Alcatraz

By the time **Theodore Cole** was sixteen years old, he had been arrested several times for grand larceny, been paroled three times, and served two years at the Oklahoma State Training School for Boys. At seventeen, he made headline news when he and accomplices attempted an armed robbery of the Dr. Pepper Bottling Works in Tulsa, Oklahoma. Cole and the others were picked up on burglary and grand larceny charges, and the authorities decided to make an example of them. Although no one died in the robbery attempt, Cole was condemned to death. However, following a public outcry, his sentence was reduced to fifteen years, and he was sent to the state prison in McAlester, Oklahoma.

In 1933, at the age of twenty-one, Cole made his first escape attempt but was foiled by a guard, who shot and wounded him as he tried to scale a prison wall. The next year, he killed his cellmate and shortly thereafter, pulled off a successful escape by hiding inside a prison laundry bag and being transported out of the prison by truck. On the run and desperate, Cole held up an unsuspecting Oklahoma farmer, James Rutherford, who had given him a ride. Cole kidnapped Rutherford and forced him to drive to Illinois, threatening his life many times during the course of the trip; he was finally caught in Dallas, Texas.

Ralph Roe left home at fourteen after losing his mother and two sisters to

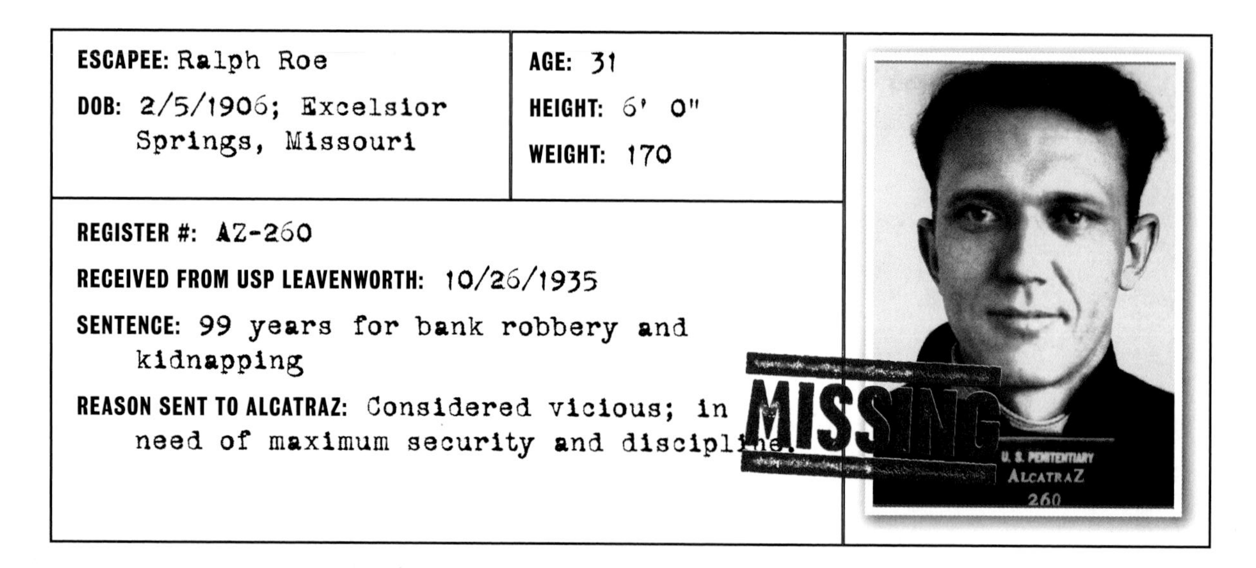

ESCAPEE: Ralph Roe

DOB: 2/5/1906; Excelsior Springs, Missouri

AGE: 31

HEIGHT: 6' 0"

WEIGHT: 170

REGISTER #: AZ-260

RECEIVED FROM USP LEAVENWORTH: 10/26/1935

SENTENCE: 99 years for bank robbery and kidnapping

REASON SENT TO ALCATRAZ: Considered vicious; in need of maximum security and discipline.

tuberculosis. He traveled across the western United States committing minor infractions and spending time in reformatories and schools for boys in California, Arkansas, and Oklahoma. Picked up and convicted numerous times for crimes ranging from robbery and grand larceny to burglary, in 1935, he hit the big time: bank robbery and kidnapping. No longer a juvenile, Roe was sentenced to ninety-nine years and sent to USP Leavenworth.

Quickly caught after his first escape, Roe was sentenced on June 28, 1927, to serve twelve years in the state prison in McAlester, Oklahoma. Two years later, he made his second escape attempt by cleverly concealing himself in an outgoing crate. Unfortunately, lack of air forced him to abandon his plan just outside the

Correctional Officer Procedures:

BAR INSPECTION

Windows and Cells, What to Look For:

1. Broken weld
2. Cracked bars
3. Cut bars

Procedures:

1. Tap end of bars, listen for distinctive rattle of bar striking against spreader plates.
2. Tap bars along length, listen for dull ring.
3. Pass a thin metal instrument, such as the back of a knife blade, along the length of bar, feeling for cuts and depressions in the bar.

Caution!

A bar that has been cut is likely to have been filled with soap, dirt, putty, etc., to conceal the cut.

United States Penitentiary
Alcatraz, California

CONDUCT REPORT

NAME Ralph Roe NO. 260-AZ.

DATE REPORTED	OFFENSE AND ACTION
1-20-36	JOINING IN STRIKE. This inmate was one of the six who went on strike from the Mat Shop. Befo**re** being questioned about returning to work, he was seen shaking his head at Kelly #49*AZ., who was goming out to be interviewed indicating to Kelly not to return to work. When brought out & asked if he was ready to return to work he refused to do so. C.J.Shuttleworth, Deputy Warden. ACTION: To be placed in open solitary D Block. C.J.Shuttleworth, Deputy Warden.
1-22-36	While officers Kranz, Morrison and myself were in the act of removing blankets from the Isolation cells this A.M. at about 7:30, the above named prisoner made the statement that "There was not enough Officers in the Institution to take his blankets and he would beat hell out of the first one that came in" The blankets were then removed with the minimum amount of force. Reported by R.O.Culver, Lieut.
1-22-36	Inmate defied guards to come in his cell after his blankets, called all guards, Deputy & Lieut. vile names whenever they approached his cell. Reported by W.B.Cotteral, Jr. C.O.
1-24-36	This prisoner is a constant noise maker, promotes discord among the other prisoners by attempting to keep them from going to work and by the use of the foulest of profane language directed at the officers. Reported by R.O.Culver, Lieut.
1-24-36	Register #260 was calling out in a very loud voice from D block to the dungeon saying #104 Conrad was on his way to the dungeon. Reported by N. Morrison, Jr. C.O.
1-24-36	Register #260 was clling out in a very loud voice, "Stick with it boys, stick with it". Reported by N. Morrison, Jr. C.O.
1-24-36	Register #260 was teling who was going back to work to some one in the cell above him (172) and calling out in a loud voice, "Don't give up boys" Reported by N. MOrrison, Jr. C.O.
1-24-36	ACTION: To solitary A block because he was continuously agitating the inmates in D block and also challenging the guards to come in and fight. C.J.Shuttleworth, Deputy Warden.
1-24-36	Talking to other inmates in solitary after being warned to stop. Reported by G.R.Boatman, Jr. C.O.
1-27-36	Dr. Jacobsen, the Deputy Warden and myself were making sick call in Solitary, when Roe's cell was opened he sat back in the corner and thumbed his nose. This was witnessed by Dr. Jacobsen, the Deputy and myself. Reported by A.E.Taylor, Jr. C.O.
1-30-36	To D block open solitary.
2-1-36	To isolation until further orders. C.J.Shuttleworth, Deputy Warden.
2-7-36	To permanent Isolation D Block at 3:00 P.M. this date C.J.Shuttleworth, Deputy Warden.
3-6-36	Roe #260-AZ. is to be removed from isolation D block to regular cell and assigned to work in the Mat Shop with the continued loss of all privileges until further orders effective 3:00 P.M. this date. C.J.Shuttleworth, Deputy Warden.

U.S.P.A.C. F. 55

Inmates transformed old tires into rubber mats for the US Navy.

prison. Granted parole in 1933, he soon allied himself with a notorious criminal, Wilber Underhill. It was during their brief association that the ruthless Underhill, Underhill's wife, and Roe's girlfriend were gunned down in a bloody shoot-out. Roe, who was wounded but survived, was convicted of harboring Underhill; released on bond—which he quickly forfeited—he was once again off and running. Still in Oklahoma, Roe (with Jack Lloyd) was recaptured while robbing the First National Bank in Sulpher. During their trial, the two men were caught plotting an escape from the jail in Muskogee.

The Plan

Cole and Roe, who had known each other as inmates at McAlester, were shipped to Alcatraz together, and once there, their register numbers—#AZ-258 and #AZ-260, respectively—put them in close proximity, which made it easier for them to hatch a plan that would make headlines across the nation. From the moment they set foot on the island, escape was on the minds of these two "Houdinis," but it would be another two years before they made their attempt. During that time, Cole and Roe learned the details of the formidable routines that ruled their lives and kept them under almost constant surveillance. They also studied the habits of individual officers, looking for opportunities to outmaneuver them and foil the system.

On the northwestern end of the island, the Model Industries Building stood atop a cliff that dropped steeply into the bay. Cole was assigned to the blacksmith shop and Roe to the adjoining mat shop on the building's ground floor, and their duties often placed them together in a back room, separated from other inmates.

Over many weeks, the men planned their breakout from this isolated location.

According to inmate Alvin Karpavicz (AKA Creepy Karpis)—who served the longest term in the history of USP Alcatraz (1936–1962)—his former crime partner, the notorious Doc Barker, was initially involved in the Cole/Roe escape. As the three men tracked the routines of the guards in their area, they realized that one guard, Junior Officer Joe Steere, often overlooked Cole and Roe. Barker decided to pull out of the plan when he realized that Cole and Roe's lucky back-room positions meant that they were the only ones who had a chance at success, since Barker's absence would quickly be noticed. (Barker made his own escape attempt two years later; see Escape File 4.)

Using a stolen hacksaw blade, Cole and Roe slowly sawed through the solid iron bars of one of the shop windows. Correctional officers were trained to inspect bars for possible tampering (see sidebar, p. 22), but certain areas were frequently missed, a fact that Cole and Roe were acutely aware of. To avoid obvious detection, they replaced missing pieces of metal with grease and shoe polish. It was speculated that Cole and Roe created floats from lightweight metal fuel cans to help them once they reached the water.

When it came time for them to break out, their plan was to loosen the precut bars and break the glass, then squeeze through the window frame, drop to the ground, and cut the chain-link fence surrounding the area, followed by a mad dash over the cliff to the water's edge.

Inmates passed through metal detectors on their way to their work assignments.

The Escape

At high noon on December 16, 1937, a dense fog enveloped San Francisco Bay. The entire prison population was in the dining hall eating their midday meal; at 12:20, when the lunch period ended, officers made a routine count of the silverware and the inmates lined up before walking single-file back to their cells. At 12:30, a head count was taken and inmates assigned to work details, including

ESCAPE FILE 2

Cole and Roe, were sent to the recreation yard to await another count. At 12:50, the inmates were led to their work posts. Cole and Roe went to their assignments; Officer Joe Steere undertook another count and found all inmates present and accounted for. Officer Steere patrolled two work areas and, as usual, at 1 PM, left one shop to oversee the other.

Cole and Roe seized the moment, quickly removing the two iron bars they had previously cut through and punching out three panes of thick glass, leaving an opening only 8.25 inches high by 17.5 inches long. One bar was bent out, the other in. Cole, a slender man, could easily slip through the space, but Roe's burly physique made it harder for him to navigate the small opening. They finally managed to get outside and, using a large Stillson wrench (which was later found at the site), broke the padlock that secured a gate in the heavy iron-mesh fence, making their way first to the cliff's edge and then to the icy bay below. The men are thought to have maneuvered down the cliff using discarded rubber from the mat shop. In moments, they entered the water and were gone.

At 1:30, when Officer Steere took the next inmate count, he discovered that

Model Industries Building, seen from the water.

Cole and Roe were not at their assigned work locations. Seeing cut bars and shards of glass, he reported them missing, and in short order, escape sirens blared across the island.

The prisoners were rushed to their cells for lockdown and guards armed with rifles boarded the island's launch and began circling the island. A large cave at the water's edge was flooded with tear gas in an attempt to flush out the escapees, but they were not found.

The Aftermath

It was hours before official word of the escape was released, but the next day as the fog lifted, the Coast Guard, Bay Area police officers, and the FBI had joined in the hunt. According to newspaper reports, six Coast Guard cutters and a police launch conducted a systematic search of the island's perimeter. Former Alcatraz inmate Blackie Audett would later write in his 1954 memoir, *Rap Sheet*, that he saw Roe struggling to stay afloat against a vicious undertow, and watched him disappear into the fog.

The currents were reported to have been particularly strong that chilly December day, and swiftly heading out to sea. James W. Bennett, director of the Bureau of Prisons, and Warden Johnston were firmly convinced that the men drowned and had no doubt been swept out to sea under the newly completed Golden Gate Bridge.

Meanwhile, police departments in the surrounding counties and the FBI followed up on every tip and rumor, with no success. From a roadhouse owner in Petaluma to a cab driver in Cole's Oklahoma hometown, false sightings poured in to police stations far and wide.

In newspapers across the nation, headlines shouted the unthinkable: two extremely dangerous criminals had escaped the nation's most secure prison. The impenetrable Alcatraz was rocked! Over the years, many outrageous stories circulated about the whereabouts of the two men. In 1941, four years after the escape, the *San Francisco Chronicle* reported that the fugitives were living comfortably in a South American hideout with plenty of money. As late as 1967, the FBI issued an internal memorandum outlining the pair's "violation" (escape) and known associates.

Did they survive? It's unlikely, but the truth will never be known.

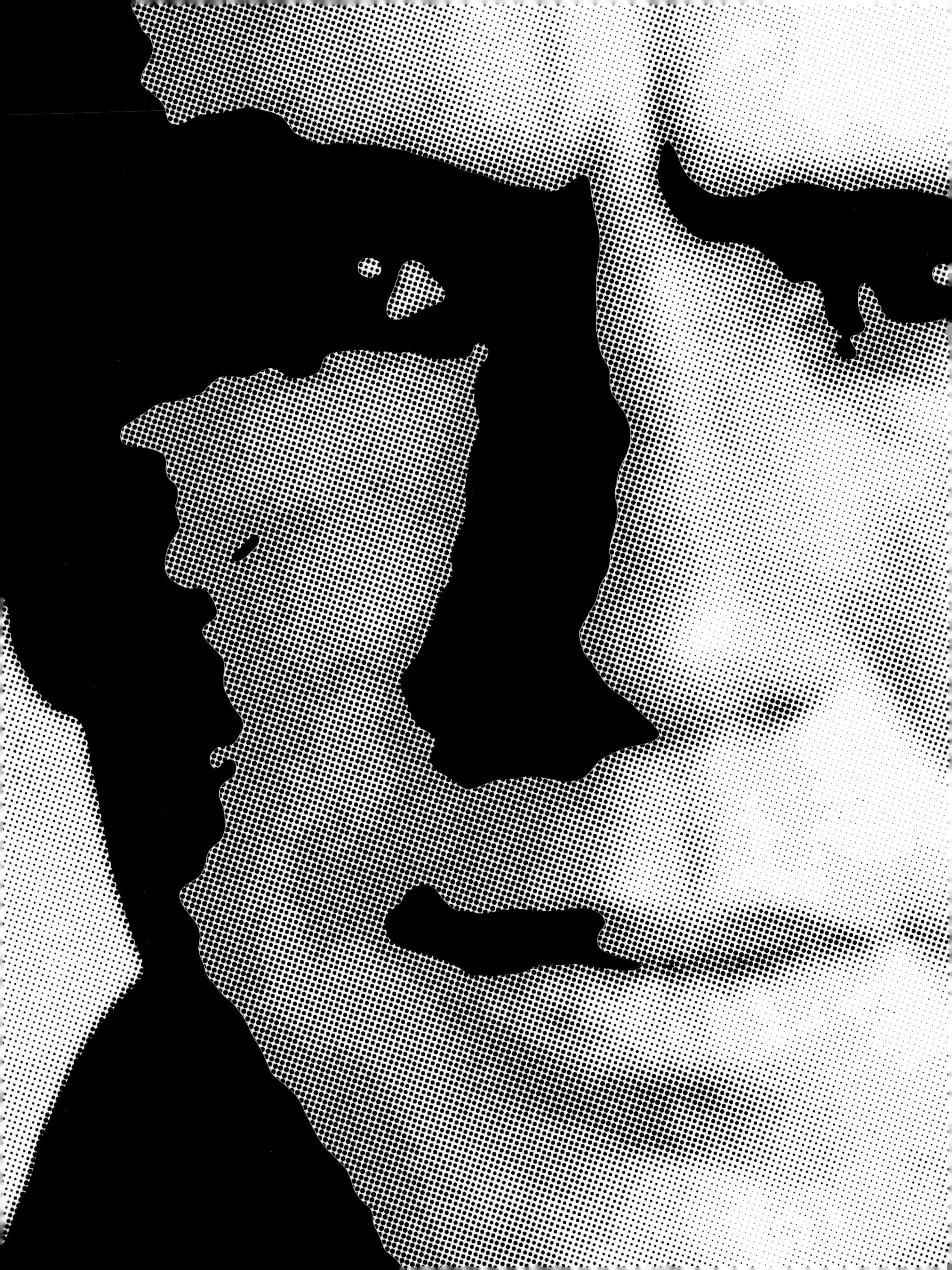

Escape 3

Desperate Escape Turns Bloody

Guard bludgeoned
to death—felon killed,
surviving inmates
charged with murder!

ESCAPE 3

DATE: May 23, 1938

LOCATION: Model Industries/Saw-filing Room

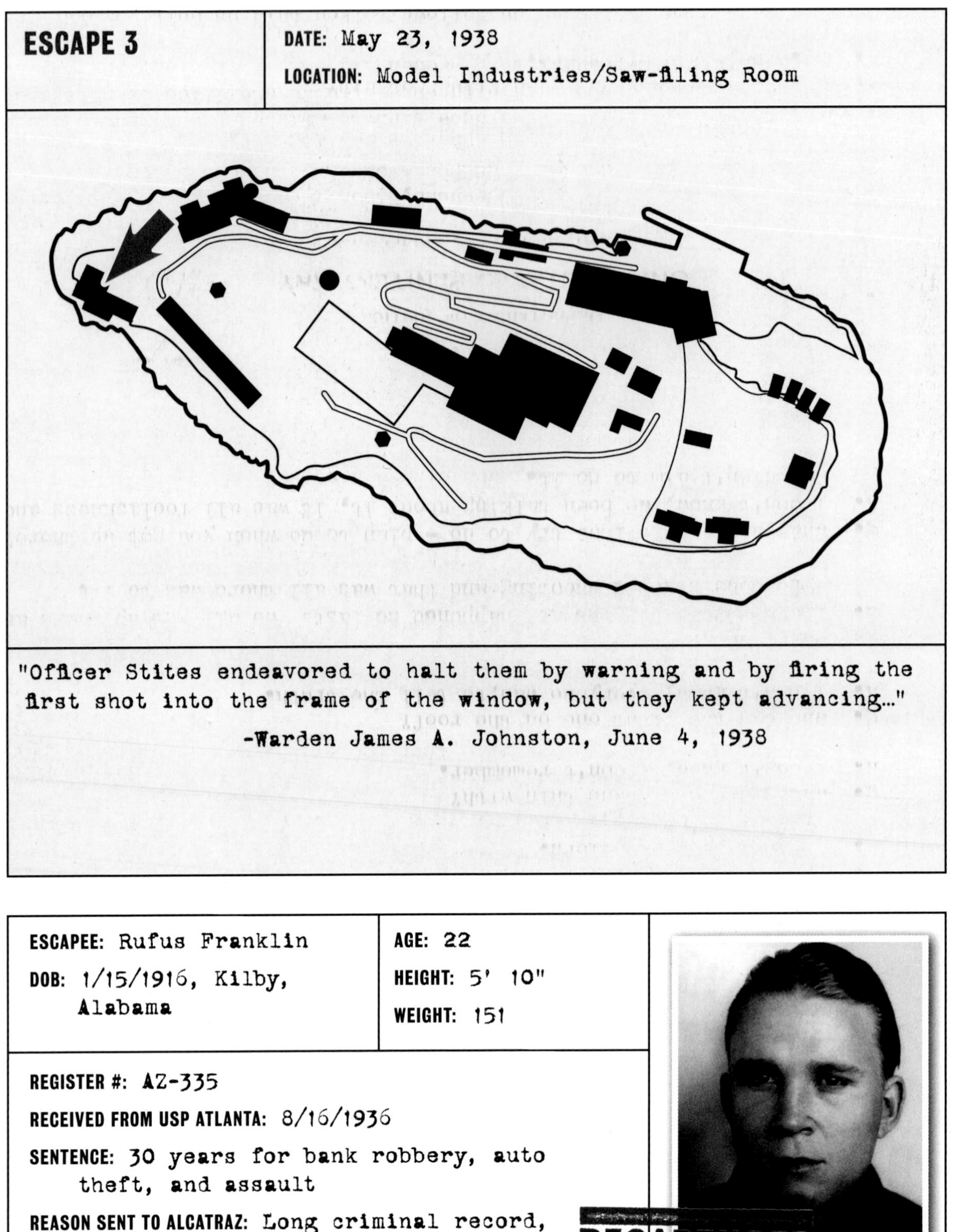

"Officer Stites endeavored to halt them by warning and by firing the first shot into the frame of the window, but they kept advancing..."

-Warden James A. Johnston, June 4, 1938

ESCAPEE: Rufus Franklin

DOB: 1/15/1916, Kilby, Alabama

AGE: 22

HEIGHT: 5' 10"

WEIGHT: 151

REGISTER #: AZ-335

RECEIVED FROM USP ATLANTA: 8/16/1936

SENTENCE: 30 years for bank robbery, auto theft, and assault

REASON SENT TO ALCATRAZ: Long criminal record, vicious demeanor, violent offenses

In the spring of 1938, three notorious bank robbers staged the first violent escape attempt the federal penitentiary had witnessed, creating a legacy of brutality that would inspire others. The bloody assault reminded the guards—and their families—of the risks they faced from men who had nothing to lose.

Road to Alcatraz

Rufus "Whitey" Franklin, one of ten children, took his first steps on a life of crime at the age of thirteen, when he stole a car and trespassed, for which he paid a $10.50 fine. His criminal career quickly escalated, and at seventeen, he was sentenced to life in prison for first-degree murder. While out of jail on a temporary release to attend his mother's funeral, Franklin added a thirty-year federal rap to his resume by robbing a bank and driving a stolen car across state lines. In 1936, Franklin was sent first to USP Atlanta and then transferred to the Rock to serve his three-decade sentence, to be followed by the earlier life sentence. Two years and one brutal escape attempt later, he added another life sentence to his record. Franklin spent a total of forty-one years in a penal institution.

The death of **Thomas Limerick**'s father, a farm-equipment mechanic in rural Nebraska, was the catalyst that launched Limerick into a life of crime. The family fell into poverty, and Limerick had to leave school and work as a laborer to support his mother and four siblings. At nineteen, he was sentenced to the Iowa State Reformatory for grand larceny; upon release, he continued his criminal ways but was caught and sentenced to the Nebraska State Penitentiary. Released once again, he committed a string of robberies. Then, on November 7, 1934, Limerick made the big leagues when he and an accomplice, armed with sawed-off shotguns, entered the First National Bank in Dell Rapids, South

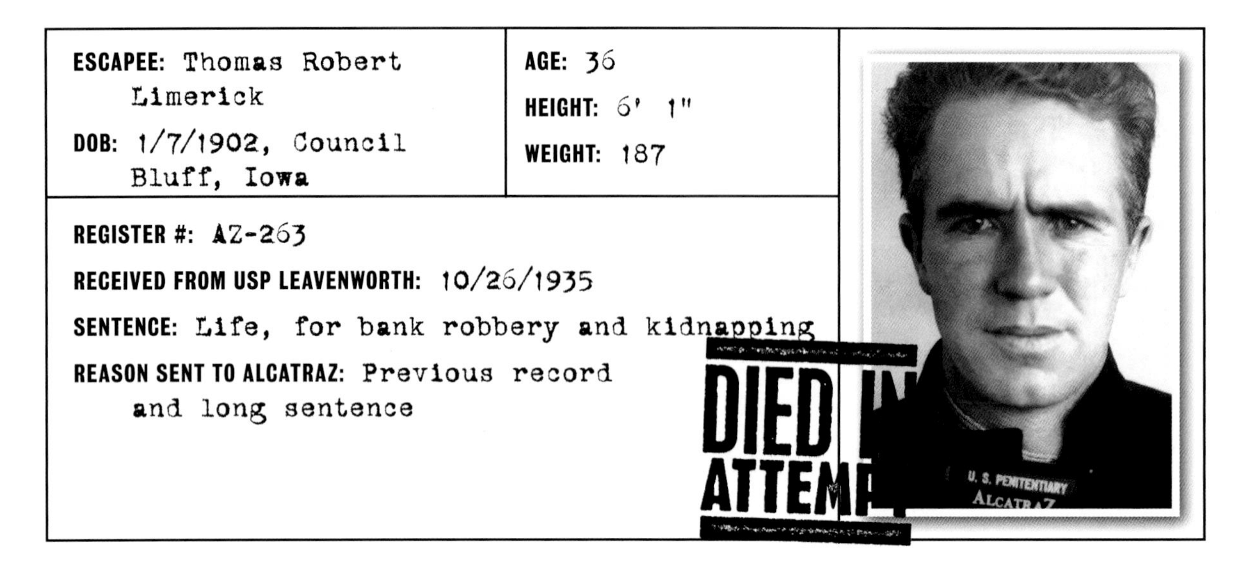
ESCAPEE: Thomas Robert Limerick

DOB: 1/7/1902, Council Bluff, Iowa

AGE: 36

HEIGHT: 6' 1"

WEIGHT: 187

REGISTER #: AZ-263

RECEIVED FROM USP LEAVENWORTH: 10/26/1935

SENTENCE: Life, for bank robbery and kidnapping

REASON SENT TO ALCATRAZ: Previous record and long sentence

Dakota, and got away with cash, stocks, and bond certificates as well as three bank employees as hostages. The following year, Limerick—by then known as the "No. 1 bank robber of the Northwest"—was captured and sentenced to life in prison. He served four months at Leavenworth before being sent to Alcatraz.

James C. "Tex" Lucas, a high-school graduate, was interested in creative writing, but ended up working in the oil fields. After his first conviction for robbery, he was sent to state prison, and shortly thereafter, made his first jailbreak. He stole a car and robbed a bank, then was captured in a gun battle and sentenced to thirty years. Lucas, one of USP Alcatraz's toughest cons, later made his prison rep by attacking mob boss Al Capone. On June 23, 1936, Lucas seized a pair of scissors in the prison barbershop, lunged ten feet across a passageway, and stabbed the notorious gangster in the back. Lurching forward, Capone screamed, then swiftly turned and punched Lucas in the jaw, sending him reeling. A guard separated the two. Capone walked to the prison hospital unassisted and returned to his regular duties the following day; Lucas went into solitary confinement. The stabbing was reportedly an outgrowth of prisoners' resentment against Capone for his refusal to join in a strike six months earlier.

Model Industries Building guard tower.

The Plan

Franklin, Limerick, and Lucas worked together in the furniture shop on the third floor of the old Model Industries

Form 792

Institution U. S. Penitentiary
Alcatraz, California

Register No. 335-AZ

REPORT ON CONVICTED PRISONER BY UNITED STATES ATTORNEY

This form is to be completed in triplicate; the yellow and blue copies to be mailed to the Warden or Superintendent of the institution to which committed, the white copy to be retained.

While this report is the only one which will be requested, the Board of Parole will appreciate receiving a report of any later facts which might bear upon the case.

By Direction of the Attorney General.

Name RUFUS FRANKLIN Age 22 Offense Murder in First Degree

Alias Robert Fraser Date of sentence November 26, 1938

Residence Anniston, Alabama Term imposed Life Imprisonment

Citizen of Alabama (County) (State) Fine: (Committed or not) No

(Post-office address) Trial Judge Judge Harold Louderback

Marital status Single Court docket no. 26334-L

Defense Attorneys Harold Faulkner and Joseph Sweeney

Appeal been filed No Date of filing

1. Did prisoner enter plea of Guilty or Not Guilty? Not Guilty Maximum term possible Death

2. Is prisoner WANTED by you or other authorities, or for deportation? By whom? For what?

No

3. Give date and details of offense committed, including any aggravating or mitigating circumstances. (Continue on separate sheet if necessary.)

7—2208

On May 23, 1938 the defendant while a prisoner at the United States Penitentiary at Alcatraz Island, California, together with James C. Lucas and Thomas R. Limerick, beat to death Royal C. Cline, Custodial officer who had been in his immediate charge. Circumstances did not indicate which of the individuals did the act but it is clear that the act was a result of their common design and in execution of their plan to escape. There were no extenuating circumstances.

4. Co-defendants (if any) and sentences imposed:

James C. Lucas - Life imprisonment in a federal penitentiary

5. Was prisoner of assistance to the Government? Explain:

No

6. Has he ever been tried on probation? Where? With what success?

No

7. Do you regard prisoner as a menace to society, an habitual criminal, an occasional offender, a victim of temptation, or a mental case? The previous criminal record of this prisoner indicates that he is an habitual criminal and at the time of this offense was serving a 30 year sentence.

8. Who are known, or suspected to be associated with him in crime?

James C. Lucas and Thomas R. Limerick

9. Against what persons should we be on guard for spurious offers of employment, or misleading statements?

Unknown

10. What reputable citizens or agencies have knowledge about the prisoner's family?

Unknown

11. Additional comment which shows the extent and intensity of public injury, or other information of use to determine parole risk: The facts indicated that the offense was cold blooded and deliberate murder and warranted the imposition of the death penalty.

12. Your comment relative to Parole:

It is the opinion of this office that under no circumstances should the prisoner be paroled.

13. The Judge's comment relative to Parole:

I ~~(do not)~~ concur in the above recommendation.

Harold Louderback
United States District Judge

Date December 12, 1938

Signed Frank J. Hennessy
FRANK J. HENNESSY, *United States Attorney*

City San Francisco

District Northern District of California

WEL:LGH

U. S. GOVERNMENT PRINTING OFFICE 7—2208

~~Def Ex # A E~~
~~Ident~~

US # 43
Evidence

DEPARTMENT OF JUSTICE

UNITED STATES PENITENTIARY

ALCATRAZ ISLAND, CALIFORNIA

May 23, 1938

Interview with inmate Lucas in Shower Room Hall by Associate Warden E. J. Miller at approximately 3:15 PM - Lieutenant Edward Starling and Foreman Plumber Klineschmidt present:

Q. (Miller) They tell me you fellows talked this up quite a bit?
A. (Lucas) Some, not much.

Q. You, Franklin and ~~[illegible]~~ Limerick, who else was there?
A. No answer.

Q. When was this first mentioned to you?
A. Darned if I know. We talked about it for four or five months.

Q. Who, just you three?
A. No.

Q. There were some others?
A. Un huh.

Q. Why did you do it?
A. Well, we just been talking about it and done it.

Q. Were you in the room when Cline got hit?
A. No. No, I wasn't there.

Q. You knew about it tho?
A. No, I didn't know.

Q. Who cut the wire?
A. I was trying to.

Q. You had the cutter?
A. I had a pair of pliers.

Q. Who did you discuss this with?
A. I don't know, I don't remember.

Q. Who was the first one on the roof?
A. I don't know, everyone was, to tell the truth.

Q. Were you first?
A. I don't remember, it all happened so fast. We all got up there and someone started shooting and that was all there was to it.

Q. What did you fellows try to do - plan to do when you got up there?
A. I don't know, we been talking about it, it was all foolishness and I didn't aim to do it.

Q. How come you didn't get shot when you got on the roof?
A. He was shooting alright and this guy run up to me and pulled a shotgun on me and told me to lay down and I sit down.

Q. You say you wasn't in the room when Cline was hit?
A. I was in the room but not when he was hit - not at the time - I went in the other room to get the pliers to cut the wire.

Q. While you were cutting the wire?
A. No, I was getting ready to start out.

Q. And you were going to take care of Mr. Cline?
A. No, I didn't know about Mr. Cline, then.

Q. What were you going to do if you got on the roof and got hold of the officer?
A. Well, we were going to try and go down to the boat.

Q. Try - you were going to try, if you got hold of the arms from the officer, to take the boat - go over the wharf and run the gun gauntlet there?
A. That was the general plan, but I thought it was foolishness to start with.

Q. You knew it was foolish but figured on going anyway?
A. I didn't want to go but had been talking about it and just went.

Q. You realize how serious it would be? Did you give it any thought?
A. A man doesn't give much thought about not doing it at the time.

----- : -----

I certify the foregoing to be a true and correct transcript of the interview.

John D. Miller
Reporter

NOTE: Above was with reference to an attempt by three inmates to attack an armed officer on the roof of the Model Bldg, secure his arms after gaining access to the roof through a window from the Furniture Factory, and escape if possible.

JDM

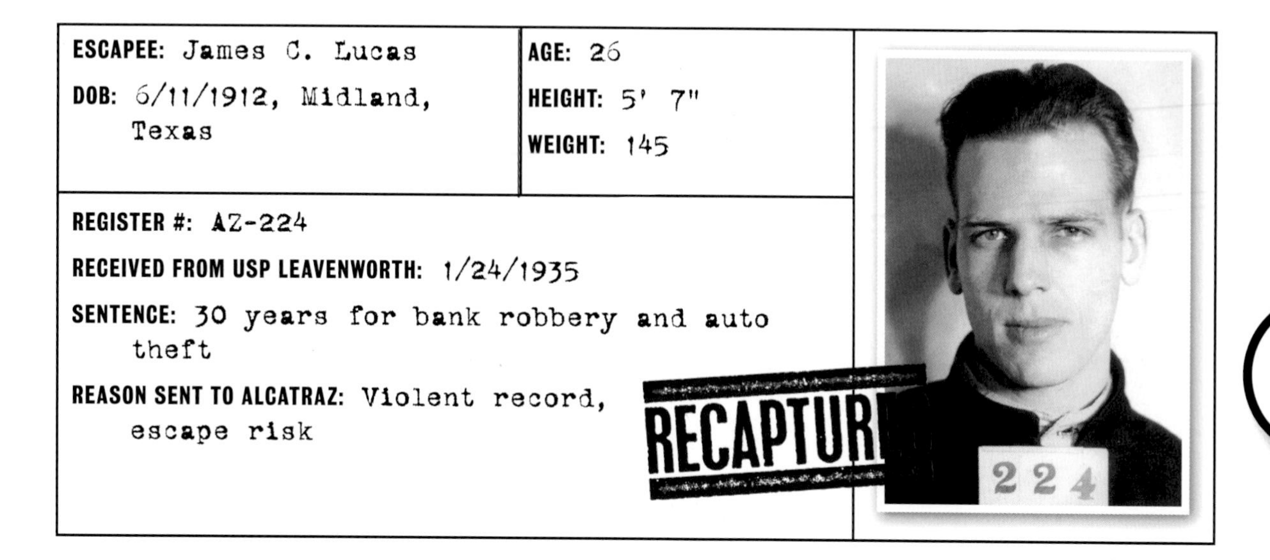

ESCAPEE: James C. Lucas
DOB: 6/11/1912, Midland, Texas
AGE: 26
HEIGHT: 5' 7"
WEIGHT: 145
REGISTER #: AZ-224
RECEIVED FROM USP LEAVENWORTH: 1/24/1935
SENTENCE: 30 years for bank robbery and auto theft
REASON SENT TO ALCATRAZ: Violent record, escape risk

Building. Their jobs gave them plenty of time to study the routines and find a weak spot to exploit. They noticed that each day after taking a count, Officer Royal C. Cline went into his office outside the workroom, and this small detail gave them the opening they needed. Once Cline went into his office, the three planned to slip through a window in the shop, climb onto the roof, attack the guard tower, and seize the officer's weapons. From there, they would advance on the catwalk from tower to tower, killing each officer and securing more weapons. Fully armed, the gang would then commandeer the prison launch and make their way to freedom.

The Escape

On May 23, 1938, shortly before two in the afternoon, the escape began as planned. Once Officer Cline stepped into his office, the convicts left their posts in the furniture shop carrying a hammer, lead weights, pliers, and some pieces of iron. They quickly snuck into the adjacent saw-filing room, where Lucas sawed a two-by-four brace, then used it to prop open a window. Then, in a heartbeat, everything changed. Officer

The furniture shop.

DEDICATED OFFICER, FAMILY MAN

Royal C. Cline, thirty-six, was specially trained in prison work and held a high rating for efficiency. He entered the federal prison service on November 24, 1931, attending the government's guard training school in New York. His first assignment was at the US Detention Farm at La Tuna, Texas. Transferred for duty to the Alcatraz penitentiary on May 13, 1934, a few weeks before it began receiving prisoners, he advanced from junior guard to the position of senior custodial officer. As Cline was a Civil Service employee, funds from the Civil Service Association's liability compensation fund were available to his widow and children, the oldest of whom was fifteen at time of his death.

Cline returned to the shop; like all correctional officers who came into direct contact with inmates, he was unarmed. Without hesitation, the three men launched a brutal attack. One of the men sunk a claw hammer into the officer's skull, and they swiftly dragged him, bleeding and unconscious, to a corner of the room. Desperate now, they pushed through the window and climbed up onto the building's roof, cutting their way through its barbed-wire perimeter.

Back on plan, Lucas approached the guard tower from the north, Limerick from the west, and Franklin from the southwest. As they stormed the tower and bombarded the glass with pieces of iron and lead, Officer Harold P. Stites—armed with a .45 automatic pistol and excellent reflexes—opened fire, hitting Limerick in the right eye. Near death, Limerick fell off the roof and plummeted to the ground. Franklin rushed the tower with his hammer. Stites, pistol empty and wounded by a piece of iron that had shattered the glass and hit him in the knee, grabbed his rifle and slammed Franklin in the shoulder. The prisoner fell into the barbed wire, a painful landing but one that saved him from plunging to his death below. Unrelenting, Lucas rushed the tower, but, alerted by Stites' gunfire, another guard patrolling the roof arrived on the scene, raised his shotgun, and took direct aim at Lucas. Cornered, Lucas raised his hands in the air and surrendered.

The Aftermath

Cline, Limerick, and Franklin were taken to the prison hospital. Limerick's wound and injuries from the fall were critical, and he died that night. Officer Cline's wounds were also severe and he was removed to the Presidio's Marine Hospital for emergency care, but it was too late; he died the next day, leaving a wife and four daughters; the American flag flew at half-staff on Alcatraz for three days. Officer Stites survived (but would not be so lucky eight years later; see Escape File 10). Franklin was under medical care for months.

ESCAPE FILE 3

Lucas and Franklin (left and center) being transported to federal court in San Francisco.

In November 1938, Franklin and Lucas went on trial for murder. Given the brutal nature of the attack on Cline, the trial was a highly charged and emotional affair. The men based their defense on the brutality that was allegedly exercised by the prison guards. Lucas claimed to have been beaten, kicked, slugged, and pushed down a flight of iron stairs at various times. He also described his imprisonment in "an old-type Spanish cage" in the black dungeon. The jury didn't buy it, and in just three weeks, the nationally publicized trial ended with convictions for first-degree murder and life sentences for both men.

AN INSIDER'S VIEW

In his book, *Alcatraz from Inside*, former inmate Jim Quillen (AZ-586), gave his opinion on the failed escape. "This escape was futile from its beginning," he said. "Even if they had obtained the weapons in the first tower, and their plans to reach the water's edge had been accomplished, there was still no possible way to escape the island. The ultimate outcome of this desperate attempt would have led to their death. However, with the killing of Officer Cline, there was no turning back, even if they did realize the impossibility of the path before them. Simply, this is what Alcatraz did to men."

Franklin spent the next few years in and out of isolation. In 1945, during a brief visit to the recreation yard, he stabbed fellow inmate Henry Young, but was not tried for the offense. Permanently released into the general population in 1954, Franklin finally adjusted and was rewarded with a job as an X-ray technician in the prison hospital. Both men were eventually transferred: Franklin was paroled from Leavenworth in 1974 and died a year later at fifty-nine, while Lucas was paroled from USP McNeil Island at the age of forty-five; according to his probation officer, "he had done an about face and became a model prisoner."

The news of the escape attempt and the death of a correctional officer at the nation's most secure prison made the pages of the *New York Times*, *Washington Post*, *Los Angeles Times*, and newspapers across the San Francisco Bay Area, shining an unwelcome spotlight on Alcatraz.

October 15, 1959

Mr. Rufus Franklin
U.S. Penitentiary
Atlanta, Georgia

Dear Rufus:

Thank you for your letter of August 9, 1959. It was a pleasure to hear from you and I know it means a great deal to you to be in Atlanta so you can receive visits from your family.

You are in a good department and your training here at Alcatraz will be helpful to you in hospital work. No doubt the Atlanta hospital is a large operation.

It has been a long time since you first came to Alcatraz and you have been through many difficult years and trials. You were a young man when you first came to us and as many young men you possessed the fire that got you into difficulty. You grew out of those years and by application improved your education and work habits. It was not easy for you since there were many pressures brought to bear that made it most difficult for you to conduct yourself as you wished to do. At any rate you accomplished what you set your mind to do and are now in a position to accomplish still more.

We hope you continue to get along well and take advantage of the many opportunities available for increased knowledge. You have learned to accept reverses gracefully and you can be a strong force in Atlanta for proper conduct and living.

I appreciate your remembering me and hope the future brings you the happiness you have missed for many years.

Sincerely,

P. J. MADIGAN
Warden

Escape 4

Bullets Fly on Bad Luck Friday

Public Enemy Doc Barker leads gang on terrifying escape.

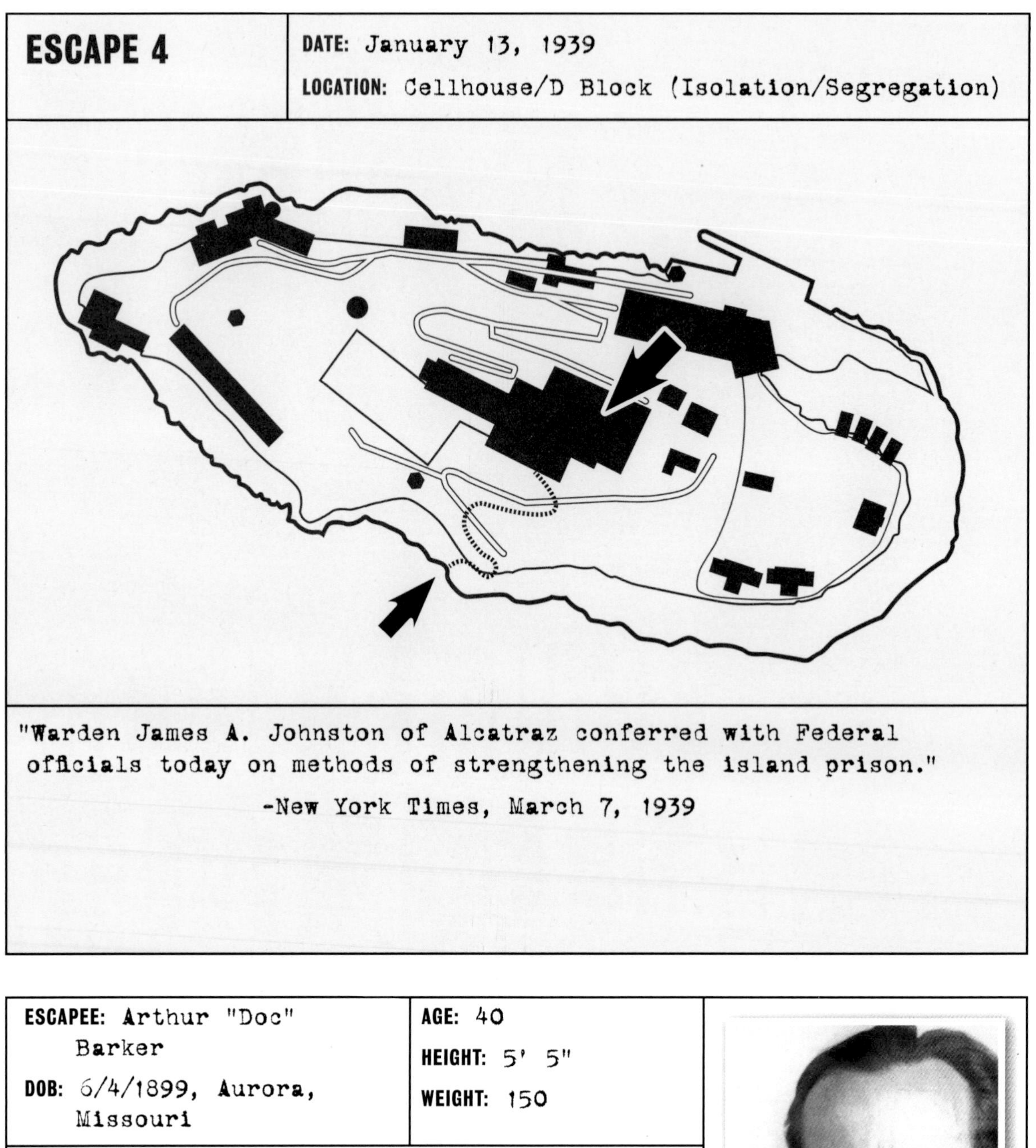

ESCAPE 4

DATE: January 13, 1939

LOCATION: Cellhouse/D Block (Isolation/Segregation)

"Warden James A. Johnston of Alcatraz conferred with Federal officials today on methods of strengthening the island prison."

-New York Times, March 7, 1939

ESCAPEE: Arthur "Doc" Barker

DOB: 6/4/1899, Aurora, Missouri

AGE: 40

HEIGHT: 5' 5"

WEIGHT: 150

REGISTER #: AZ-268

RECEIVED FROM USP LEAVENWORTH: 10/26/1935

SENTENCE: Life in prison for kidnapping

REASON SENT TO ALCATRAZ: Aggressive behavior, violent crimes, escape risk

DIED IN ATTEM

The Barker-Karpis gang was one of the most notorious criminal outfits of the 1930s. Alvin (Creepy) Karpis and Ma Barker's sons terrorized the Midwest, robbing banks, kidnapping wealthy citizens for ransom, and murdering those who got in their way. Not long after Doc Barker found himself behind bars at Alcatraz, he began plotting his escape.

Road to Alcatraz

Arthur "Doc" Barker, born in Missouri's Ozark Mountains, was the third of four sons of the infamous Kate "Ma" Barker and miner George Barker. Though the story put out by the FBI credited Ma with being the criminal mastermind of the Barker-Karpis gang, Alvin Karpis debunked that as a myth: "Ma Barker . . . wasn't a leader of criminals or even a criminal herself. . . . She knew we were criminals, but her participation in our careers was limited to one function: when we traveled together, we moved as a mother and her sons. What could look more innocent?" Bank robber Harvey Bailey, who also served time at Alcatraz between 1934 and 1946, said in his autobiography that Ma Barker "couldn't plan breakfast," much less a heist or a kidnapping.

Like his three brothers—Herman, Lloyd, and Fred—Barker started young as a petty thief. The police regularly rounded up Arthur and his brothers and took them to jail, which caused his mother to complain, "They're marked! The cops here won't ever stop persecuting my boys." Looking for a place where they weren't as well known, Ma moved her brood to Tulsa, Oklahoma, where the boys formed the Central Park Gang. In 1918, after being arrested for stealing a government vehicle, Doc escaped from the Tulsa County Jail and spent the next two years working undetected as a glass blower and laborer. Eventually, he was discovered and returned to the Tulsa County Jail, then released within the year.

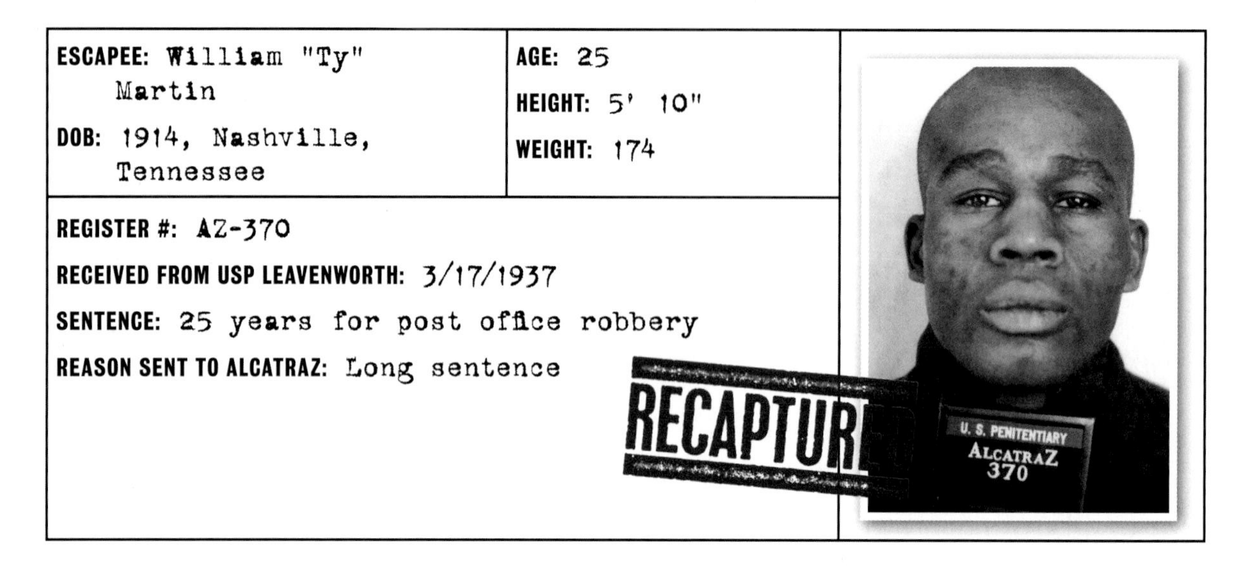

ESCAPEE: William "Ty" Martin

DOB: 1914, Nashville, Tennessee

AGE: 25

HEIGHT: 5' 10"

WEIGHT: 174

REGISTER #: AZ-370

RECEIVED FROM USP LEAVENWORTH: 3/17/1937

SENTENCE: 25 years for post office robbery

REASON SENT TO ALCATRAZ: Long sentence

Barker's life of crime continued apace, with occasional interruptions for incarceration. No matter what the crime—be it bank robbery or murder—Ma spent years trying to convince officials of her son's innocence. On condition that he leave the state, Barker was paroled in 1932, allegedly through bribery of state officials. In 1934, Barker went through an intensely painful operation to have his fingerprints obliterated. This didn't help, however, when he, his mother, his brother Fred, Alvin Karpis (who also wound up at Alcatraz), and several others kidnapped Edward Bremer, president of the Commercial State Bank in St. Paul, Minnesota. Once captured, he was sentenced to life, shipped to Leavenworth in May 1935, and transferred to Alcatraz five months later.

William "Ty" Martin, raised by his father and stepmother, had his first brush with crime at fifteen. Convicted of robbery, he was sentenced to the reformatory in Pontiac, Illinois, and was later transferred to Joliet Penitentiary. Upon his release in 1936, he almost immediately robbed a post office in Chicago of $120.17. A powerfully built man, Martin was described as bitter and unstable; he admitted to officials that upon his release, he would rob a bank or other business rather than seek gainful employment. Martin's mother had been declared insane when Martin was a child, and in 1938, his own mental competence had been questioned; however, the chief medical officer who examined him then found no evidence of psychosis.

Rufus McCain was the youngest in a family of seven children. Raised by his father and stepmother, he finished eighth grade at the age of seventeen and struck out on his own to work as an oil driller and farmer. Until he was in his early thirties, McCain lived a predictable middle-class life. Then he robbed an Indian grave and received a stint in the Oklahoma State Penitentiary, which was

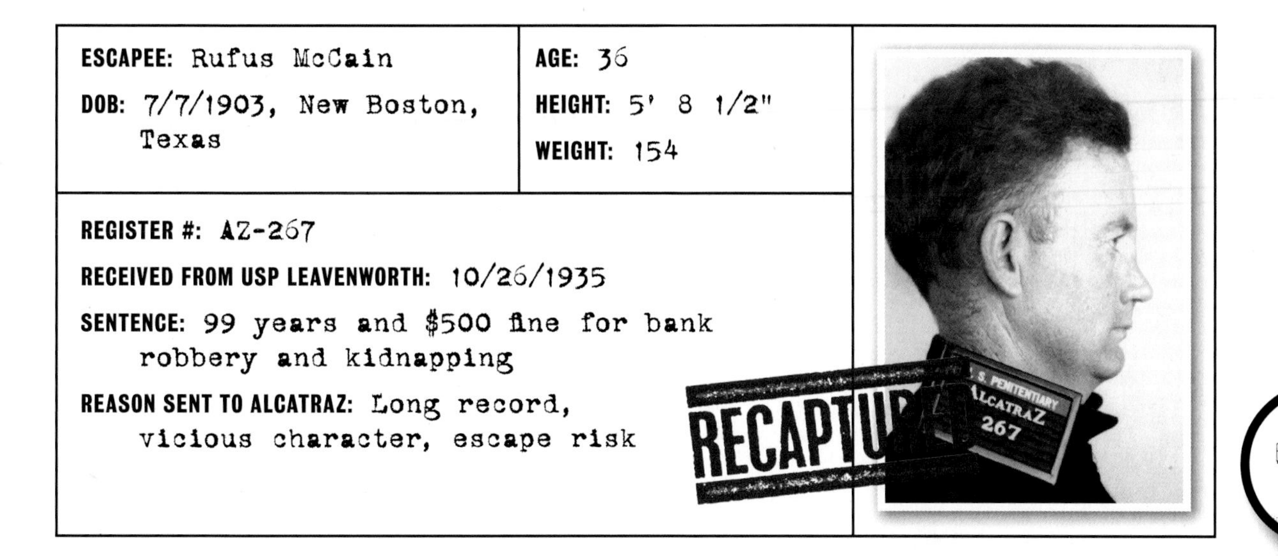
ESCAPEE: Rufus McCain

DOB: 7/7/1903, New Boston, Texas

AGE: 36

HEIGHT: 5' 8 1/2"

WEIGHT: 154

REGISTER #: AZ-267

RECEIVED FROM USP LEAVENWORTH: 10/26/1935

SENTENCE: 99 years and $500 fine for bank robbery and kidnapping

REASON SENT TO ALCATRAZ: Long record, vicious character, escape risk

followed by time in the Arkansas State Penitentiary for robbery and assault to kill. In April 1935, McCain made a successful jailbreak, and a short time later, he and Samuel Marion Day robbed the Idabel National Bank in Oklahoma. The caper netted the pair $2,600. Fleeing with the money, they took two bank employees as hostages. Day died in the gun battle that broke out when the police caught up with the men, and McCain faced federal charges on his own. Though he was initially sent to Leavenworth, officials took his record, his escape, and the violence that had capped his last offense into account and decided to ship him to maximum-security Alcatraz. McCain arrived on the same train of prisoners that brought Arthur "Doc" Barker, and it's likely that he met Barker at Oklahoma State Penitentiary while McCain was serving time for "interference with the place of burial" and Barker was serving time for the murder he insisted he didn't commit. McCain was a difficult and violent prisoner. During his time on the Rock, he attacked an inmate with a homemade knife, was frequently cited for agitating prisoners and creating disturbances, and was found drunk and in possession of contraband, forfeiting a total of 11,880 days (over thirty-two years) of statutory good time for his behavior.

Kidnapper and bank robber **Dale Stamphill** was arrested and convicted in 1937 at the age of twenty-five and imprisoned at the state reformatory in Granite, Oklahoma. While there, Stamphill and twenty-one other prisoners escaped after killing a tower guard. He and two accomplices later robbed the First National Bank in Seiling, Oklahoma, during which one of the men was injured. Stamphill then kidnapped a doctor at gunpoint from his home and forced him to treat the injured man. Finally captured in Texas, Stamphill received a life sentence for the guard's murder and was sent to USP Leavenworth. His history of escapes earned

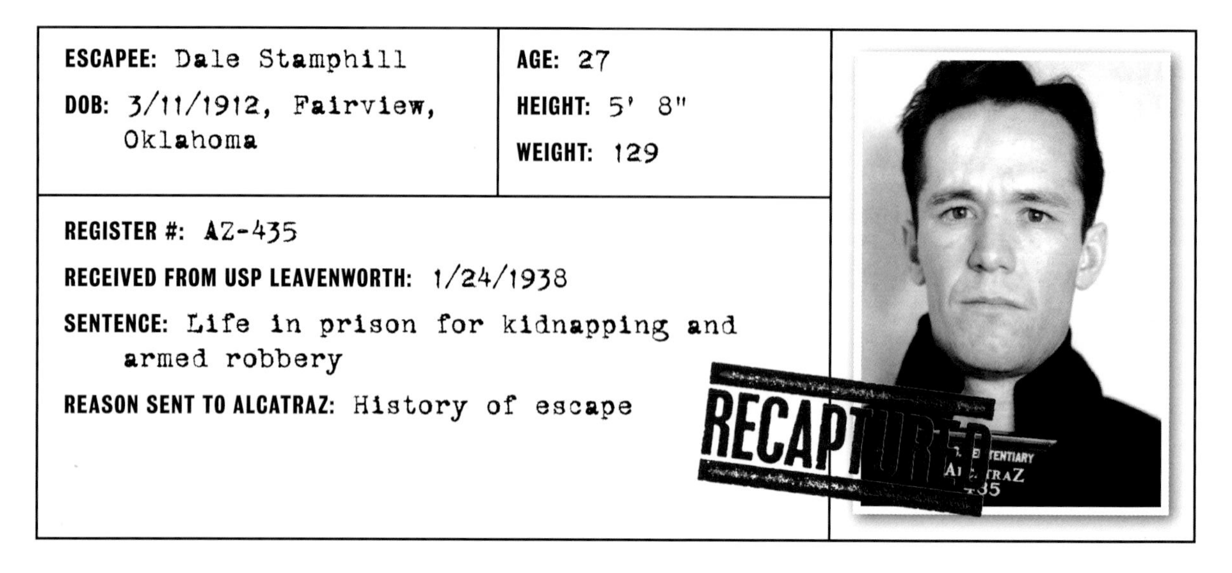
ESCAPEE: Dale Stamphill
DOB: 3/11/1912, Fairview, Oklahoma
AGE: 27
HEIGHT: 5' 8"
WEIGHT: 129
REGISTER #: AZ-435
RECEIVED FROM USP LEAVENWORTH: 1/24/1938
SENTENCE: Life in prison for kidnapping and armed robbery
REASON SENT TO ALCATRAZ: History of escape

him a transfer to Alcatraz the next year. Stamphill spent virtually all of his adult life in prison, except for a ten-year period during which he worked (under parole supervision) as a tax accountant. He was considered the best worker in the Alcatraz tailor shop and received excellent reports for his work and cooperative attitude in the library, clothing room, and laundry.

Henry Young was among the most incorrigible and infamous prisoners confined to Alcatraz. Young's childhood was spent in poverty, with his parents fighting constantly; as a youngster, he was taught to how to steal by his machinist father. Henry's parents divorced when he was fourteen, and three years later, his mother remarried a man with six children. Unable to get along with his new stepfather, Young left home, taking odd jobs and launching a crime spree throughout the West. After a series of burglaries, robberies, and kidnappings, Young robbed the First National Bank of Lind, Washington; he and his confederates made off with only $405. Captured within thirty minutes, he received a twenty-year sentence and was shipped to USP McNeil Island. Officials pleaded for his transfer to Alcatraz, one attorney calling him "the worst and most dangerous criminal with whom I've ever dealt, although I have prosecuted and hung two individuals on the charge of murder." The warden at McNeil Island agreed: "He is vicious, unscrupulous, and a fomenter of trouble."

On Alcatraz, Young received thirty-four write-ups for misconduct, the first just a month after he arrived on the island—among them, loud laughing, talking at mess, refusing to work, wasting food, smoking in the gallery, possession of contraband, joining in strike, suspected of sabotage, fighting, refusing to leave his cell, yelling threats, causing confusion, destroying government property, trading fountain pens, attempting to escape, cursing, stabbing an inmate, and

Administrative Form No. 16
March, 1938

FOR VICTORY BUY UNITED STATES WAR BONDS AND STAMPS

INTRA-BUREAU CORRESPONDENCE

UNITED STATES DEPARTMENT OF JUSTICE
UNITED STATES BUREAU OF PRISONS
UNITED STATES PENITENTIARY
ALCATRAZ, CALIFORNIA

DEPARTMENT OF JUSTICE
BUREAU OF PRISONS
1947 AUG 18 PM 3 49

TO: A. H. Conner, Acting Director DATE August 12, 1947

RE: Mail

IN REPLY REFER TO:

For your information I am enclosing copy of letter mailed by William Dainard, Reg. No. 477-AZ to Senator William Langer, by Henri Young, Reg. No. 244-AZ to Senator Langer, by Ollie O. Melton, Reg. No. 777-AZ to Senator Langer, and by Richard A. Numer, Reg. No. 286-AZ to Senator Kenneth McKellar.

It appears that one of the national magazines, I think it was "The Pathfinder" printed an item to the effect that Senator Langer intends to visit and inspect all of the Federal Prisons. No doubt more prisoners will write to him for an interview and a chance to tell their troubles. In the circumstances I will mail such letters directly to the Senator, because it is apparent that complaints are welcomed and perhaps encouraged, and that being the case I think the inmates ought to have a chance to make them and the Senator an opportunity to check them.

J. A. JOHNSTON
Warden

COPY

FROM: Henri Young, 244-AZ
Alcatraz, California

August 10, 1947

TO : Senator William Langer, Washington, D. C

Dear Sir:

I have learned thru news publications that you are preparing to investigate the federal prisons for administrative abuses. As this objective will bring you to Alcatraz, I should be happy to obtain a private interview with you so as to furnish you with unequivocal proof of administrative economic stupidity here.

Your publicised ridicule of the loan to Britian was highly pleasing to me. On a smaller scale, I can furnish you with a pot full of ridicule to dish out to the public of the disgusting and costly economic idiocies committed here at Alcatraz.

I hope to remain, Sir.

Most respectfully yours,

/s/ Henri Young, 244-AZ

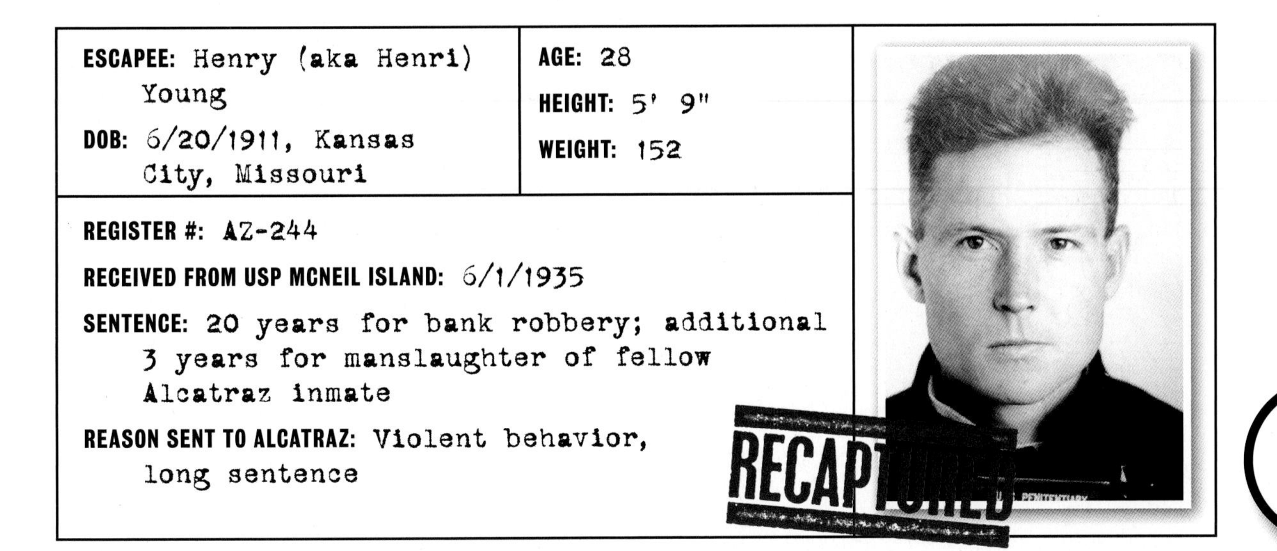

ESCAPEE: Henry (aka Henri) Young

DOB: 6/20/1911, Kansas City, Missouri

AGE: 28

HEIGHT: 5' 9"

WEIGHT: 152

REGISTER #: AZ-244

RECEIVED FROM USP MCNEIL ISLAND: 6/1/1935

SENTENCE: 20 years for bank robbery; additional 3 years for manslaughter of fellow Alcatraz inmate

REASON SENT TO ALCATRAZ: Violent behavior, long sentence

RECAPTURED

disregarding the rule of silence. Again and again, Young would be moved to isolation. Once he learned of Doc Barker's plan to break the Rock, he was eager to join in.

The Plan

Working with Stamphill, whose job assignment—delivering library books—gave him both unobstructed access to most of the cellhouse and a way to receive and transport contraband tools, Barker devoted himself to recruiting accomplices, studying the Rock's security system and guard routines, and developing an escape plan. Barker and Stamphill carefully analyzed the two earlier breakouts from the Model Industries Building during daylight hours: the "successful" escape by Cole and Roe, and the disastrous attempt by Limerick, Franklin, and Lucas. Eventually, they determined that the best place from which to make a break was where Warden Johnston and the guards considered the prison to be the most secure: D Block. They knew that the bars of the isolation unit's cells were made of flat, soft iron (a holdover from the island's years as a military prison, 1912–1933), not the tool-proof hardened-steel bars used on cell doors in B and C Blocks. This meant that the bars could be more easily sawed through.

As part of the plan, each man had to create an incident that would get him thrown into one of the D Block isolation cells. Once that had been accomplished, they worked diligently for weeks, quietly sawing through the bars of their cells using tools other inmates smuggled to them. The windows of D Block, which were protected by tool-proof bars, posed a more complicated obstacle, but it too was overcome, thanks to a bar-spreader manufactured by an inmate who worked

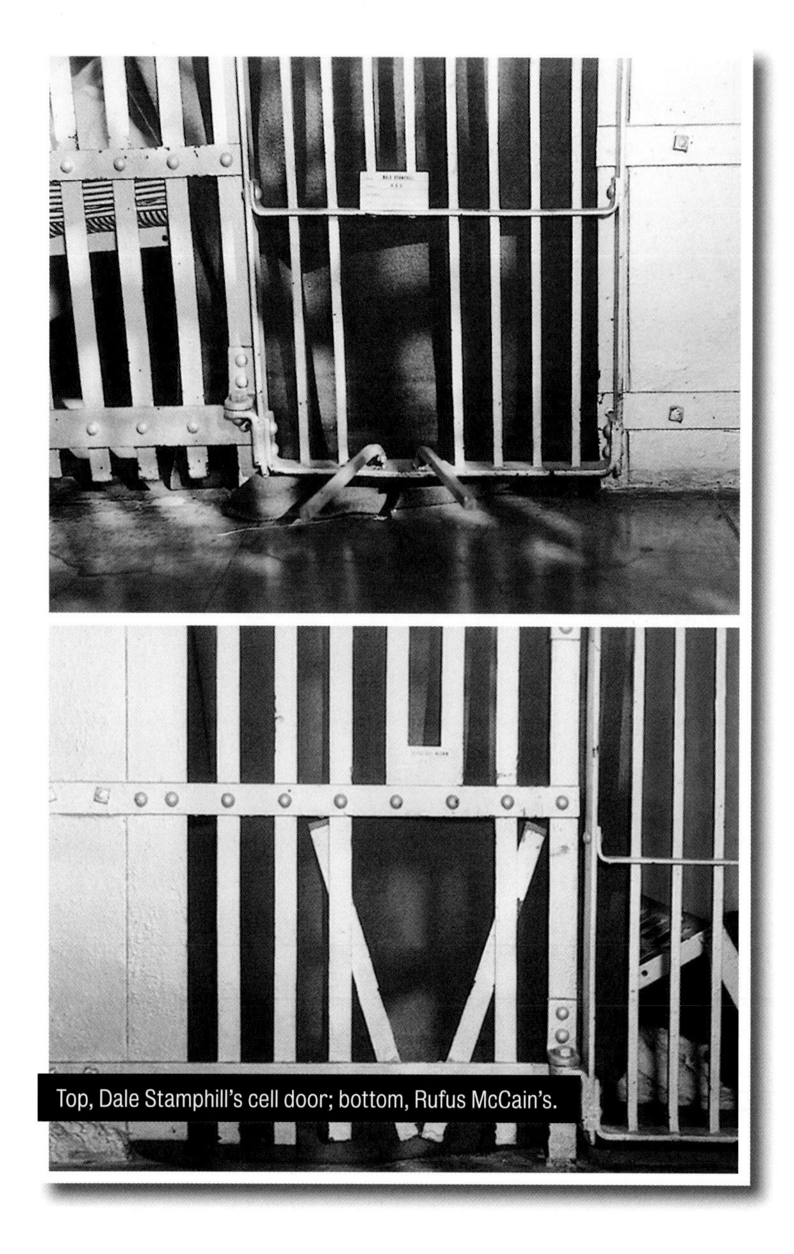
Top, Dale Stamphill's cell door; bottom, Rufus McCain's.

in one of the Model Industries shops. While the rest of the general prison population was in the dining hall, two of the conspirators pushed aside the loose bars on their cell doors and employed the bar spreader to break the bars over the windows. Using putty and cement, they set the bars back in place and waited for the signal to escape.

The Escape

A heavy fog covered Alcatraz in the early-morning hours of Friday, January 13, 1939. The conspirators, who knew that only one guard would be on duty after midnight, waited until 3 AM—between guard tours—to make their move. Taking their bed sheets with them, they spread open the pre-sawed bars of their cell doors, crossed the empty corridor, pried loose the window bars, and struggled through the window, dropping onto the roadway eight feet below. The mist obscured their movements as they quickly made their way to the edge of the island, picking up bits of scrap lumber along the way. When they reached their destination, the men split up. Martin started to climb down a twenty-foot cliff, while McCain and Young, using improvised tools and haphazard supplies, constructed a crude raft at the edge of a small beach on the island's rocky shoreline. Stamphill and Barker followed concrete steps to the water's edge and plunged in.

Time quickly ran out for the escapees. At 3:45 AM, the empty cells were discovered, and almost immediately, the siren sounded, the prison launch set out to patrol the shoreline, and searchlights flashed on. For a moment, the fog lifted, and guards standing on the cliff above the cove saw Stamphill and Barker entering the water; they sprayed the area with machine-gun and rifle fire. Barker took

HENRY YOUNG'S ACCOUNT

"My heart was in my mouth. I felt strange, nervous, like a man in a dream. On the beach we hurriedly threw together a makeshift raft, tying the lumber we had gathered with the sheets we carried. We stripped and made bundles of our clothes and put them on the raft. We swam out, pushing the raft before us. Thirty yards out, McCain called a halt. He said that the raft was weak, in danger of falling apart. He insisted on going back for more lumber to strengthen our raft."

The cove, later called "Barker Beach."

April 23, 1940

TO: J. A. Johnston, Warden

FROM: E. J. Miller, Associate Warden

RE: #370-Az Martin

This man is confined in "D" Block Isolation and has been there since attempted escape on January 13, 1939. A few weeks ago he went on what we might call a "small hunger strike". He would not eat for a few days, then suddenly begin to eat again, not giving any clear reason for his actions, saying only that he thought it would do him some good. On April 15, 1940 this man again refused his meals and upon talking to him could get no reason for his refusal of meals. He merely said that he was all right. I interviewed him each time I went through Isolation on inspection and always got the same answer from him. On the morning of April 23, 1940, while making my regular trip through Isolation, Martin began to talk to me telling me that the fellows were hissing him and calling him a rat. According to his story, they figured he had "snitched" on them so they began to hiss him, call him names, and tell him what they were going to do to him, etc. After asking why he was not eating again, he said he thought that by not eating they might stop calling him names. He said they were leading up to the point where they will have the entire cell house hissing at him. Said he would like to be moved from there, as he would not like to hurt anybody or get hurt. Told him he would have to stay in Isolation a long time and that I did not know of any place where he could "cell away" from this particular group of men. I said I thought he was foolish not to eat. Today he ate his noon meal. I have not interviewed him since.

direct hits to his head and thigh, and Stamphill had bullet wounds in both legs. Navigating into the cove in a small rowboat, guards hoisted the two wounded men aboard and transported them back to the prison hospital. Martin—clad only in socks in the bitterly cold night air—fell from his perch on the cliff and was badly bruised on the rocks; he was also picked up and taken to the hospital. McCain and Young were found shivering in their underwear; they surrendered peacefully. Though the Alcatraz hospital was equipped for emergencies, Barker was beyond help and died that night. His last words were said to have been, "I was a fool to try it. I'm all shot to hell."

The Aftermath

Sensational newspaper reports covered nearly every aspect of the attempted escape, including the many shortcomings in the prison's operations. Associate Warden Miller admitted that officers on duty in the cellhouse might have been asleep during the breakout, but this was never proven. Given the number of tools that the escapees had access to, it was also clear that the metal detector wasn't doing its job; further investigation revealed that it worked only about 60 percent of the time.

Citizens and public officials alike were outraged over what they saw as ineffective security procedures on the Rock. In a press conference, Attorney General Frank Murphy said, "It is a great injustice to San Francisco to have that place of horror on the doorstep of the city. . . . The whole institution is conducive to psychology that builds up a sinister and vicious attitude among prisoners. . . . It won't be changed until something better in the public interest is arranged."

Both Stamphill and Martin recovered from their injuries. According to Alcatraz officials, Stamphill "steadied down" after the 1939 attempt and was recommended for transfer to Leavenworth. After being paroled in 1956, he married and lived a conventional life, starting a tax and accounting firm. Then, deeply in debt, he bungled a burglary and found himself back in prison.

Martin, on the other hand, went downhill, and by 1940, his mental state was clearly in decline. He gave paranoid explanations of his difficulties, claimed to be a licensed surgeon

ALCATRAZ ON TRIAL

In April 1941, Henry Young went on trial for the murder of Rufus McCain. Young was represented by two youthful attorneys who shifted the trial's focus from the crime to the prison's conditions and treatment of the entire inmate population. Twenty-two Alcatraz prisoners testified in Young's defense, many of whom insisted that they'd also been beaten by the guards. Others reported that McCain had been out to get Young. The defense strategy prevailed, and a sympathetic jury returned a verdict of manslaughter. Furious with the outcome, the judge gave Young the maximum sentence: three additional years on the Rock. In 1948, Young was transferred to the federal medical facility at Springfield, Missouri, where he stayed for six years before being handed over to the state of Washington to serve time at the state penitentiary at Walla Walla for a murder he committed in 1935. Paroled in 1972, he disappeared and was never heard from again.

and Oxford graduate, said officers and doctors were people he had known in the past, and even referred to one of them as his brother-in-law. He admitted he could hear "voices," refused food on various occasions, and would often strip off all his clothing. In 1941, he was declared schizophrenic and transferred to the Medical Center for Federal Prisoners (MCFP) in Springfield, Missouri.

After the failed attempt, Young was returned to isolation and forfeited 2,400 days of statutory good time. Almost immediately after rejoining the general population, he unleashed his fury on Rufus McCain, whom he blamed for their capture. On December 3, 1940, Young pulled out two sharpened knives from their hiding place under a lathe near his work station, slipped out of the shop, walked down a flight of stairs, and entered the tailor shop where McCain was working. Running to up McCain, he stabbed him, twisting the blade deep into McCain's gut. It took McCain six hours to die in the prison hospital. In the sensational murder trial that followed, Alcatraz itself was blamed for the murder (see sidebar on p. 55).

The tailor shop.

Form 9501
U. S. TREASURY DEPARTMENT
PUBLIC HEALTH SERVICE
Penal and Correctional Institutions
July, 1931

IN-PATIENT MEDICAL RECORD

CLINICAL BRIEF

BRIEF (1)

Date Jan. 14, 1939

1-13-39 5:15 AM C BARKER, Arther 269Az
Date and hour admitted to HOSPITAL: Date of expected discharge from INSTITUTION: Ward assigned: Name (surname first, in capitals) Register number

NEW INMATE : SICK LINE : AFTER SICK LINE : NIGHT ROUNDS : AMBULATORY : ASSISTED : STRETCHER X :
Source of present hospital admission Condition on admission to the hospital

ILLNESS : OBSERVATION PHYSICAL X : OBSERVATION MENTAL : STUDY : REMEDIABLE DEFECT : INJURY X: DENARCOTIZATION :
Reason for admission to the hospital

DURING ENTIRE LIFE : DURING PRESENT SENTENCE : DURING CURRENT FISCAL YEAR :
Number of hospital admissions, INCLUDING THE PRESENT ONE Number of out-patient calls made this sentence

S M W D SEP DES : W N M I C O : Okla. W M 39 P C J OTHER NONE : YES NO :
Marital status : Color : Nativity : Race : Sex : Age : Religion : Narcotic addiction : Number of children

Laborer
Former occupation Institution occupation Cell location

Does patient desire any change in previously expressed wishes regarding persons to be notified if he becomes seriously ill?

[signature]
Admitting Officer.

(NOTE—In entering diagnoses below, first give those that are significant to his present hospital admission in the order of their importance; then leave a blank space and list those that were found previously, but this time in the numerical order in which they appear in the NOMENCLATURE.)

NUMBER	DISEASE OR CONDITION	DATE	CONDITION ON DISPOSITION
4063	Fracture, compound, Skull	1-13-39	Dead
4063	Fracture, compound, left femur	"	"
4126	Wound, gunshot, head, left femur, and right eye.	"	"
	Complications or sequelae		
178	Operations Fracture, compound, treatment, Thomas splint left leg.	1-13-39	Dead

RETURNED TO DUTY : LIGHT DUTY : QUARTERS FOR DAYS : IDLE : TRANSFERRED TO
Disposition

1-13-39 1 : DIED 5:40PM 1-13-39 Skull fracture. : AUTOPSY; YES NO
Date of disposition Number of days in the Hospital:

[signature]
CA Surgeon.

[initials]

Escape 5

Motorboat Escape Plan Stuns Prison

4 guards taken hostage as desperate inmates saw through bars.

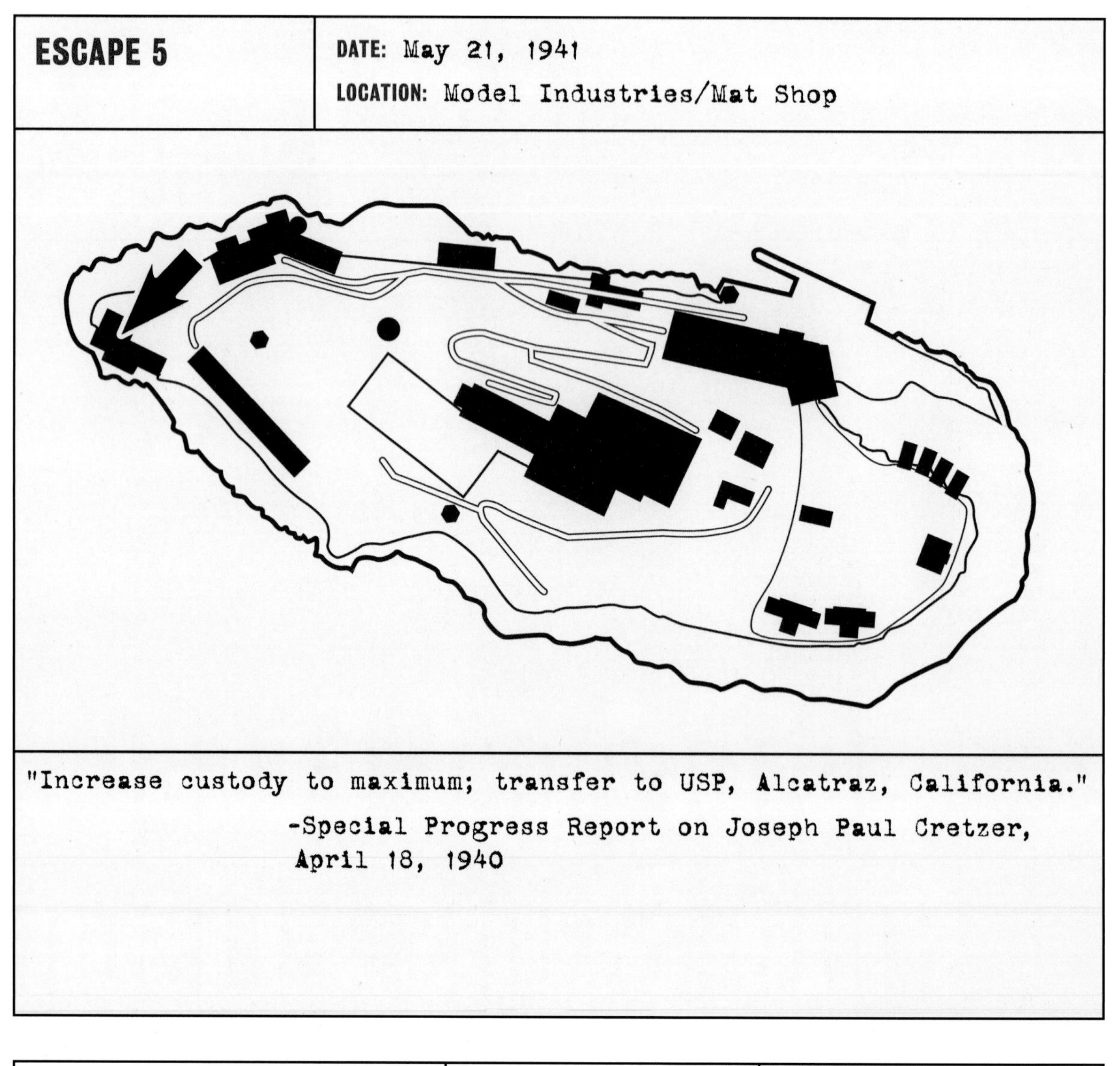

ESCAPE 5

DATE: May 21, 1941

LOCATION: Model Industries/Mat Shop

"Increase custody to maximum; transfer to USP, Alcatraz, California."

-Special Progress Report on Joseph Paul Cretzer, April 18, 1940

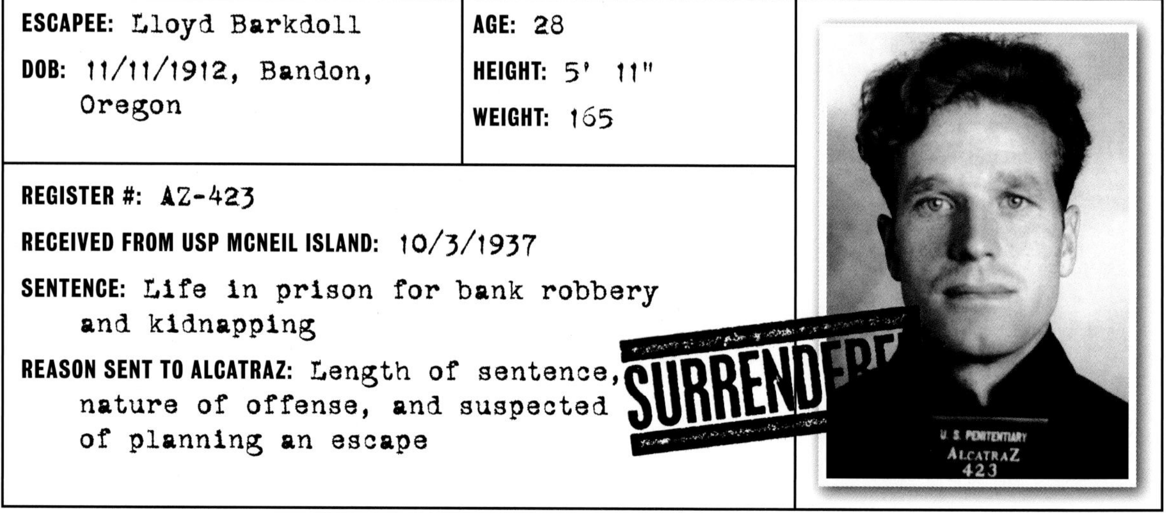

ESCAPEE: Lloyd Barkdoll

DOB: 11/11/1912, Bandon, Oregon

AGE: 28

HEIGHT: 5' 11"

WEIGHT: 165

REGISTER #: AZ-423

RECEIVED FROM USP MCNEIL ISLAND: 10/3/1937

SENTENCE: Life in prison for bank robbery and kidnapping

REASON SENT TO ALCATRAZ: Length of sentence, nature of offense, and suspected of planning an escape

Each of these dangerous felons was imprisoned for life. They had no hope for a pardon or parole, and they had nothing left to lose. Two were infamous partners in crime; on the outside, Cretzer and Kyle were a bank-robbing duo (and brothers-in-law). Inside, they were on the same work detail.

Road to Alcatraz

Lloyd Barkdoll, who said that he enjoyed the thrill of theft more than the money he stole, was convicted of larceny numerous times and spent time in the Oregon State Training School and Oregon State Penitentiary. In 1937, he and two accomplices kidnapped a bank cashier from his home and forced him to go to the Grant County Bank in John Day, Oregon, and open the doors and vault. The men got away with more than $3,000, but didn't have much time to

THE ROCK ISLANDERS

Lloyd Barkdoll led the prison orchestra, the Rock Islanders; John Bayless, another prisoner who attempted to escape (Escape File 6) was among the band members.

enjoy it. When their getaway car crashed in a culvert, Barkdoll flagged down a passing motorist and took his car. Two days later, he was arrested in Portland, Oregon. Convicted of bank robbery and kidnapping, he was sentenced to prison for life and received at USP McNeil Island in July 1937; not long after, he found himself on his way to Alcatraz. He had a short reprieve from the Rock when he was later transferred to Leavenworth. Claiming to have information about another kidnapping, Barkdoll made a deal with the Department of Justice to reveal all he knew in return for a sentence reduction to twenty-five years and the move the Kansas. When it became apparent he did not have—or would not reveal—information about that crime, he was returned to Alcatraz. Officials speculated that he may have made up the story to gain an opportunity to escape during the transfer.

Joe "Dutch" Cretzer was born to deaf-mute parents; the family moved to Oakland, California, when he was ten. Eventually, his parents divorced and his mother remarried, but Joe did not get along with his new stepfather. Beginning at age fourteen, Cretzer followed the criminal path of his two older brothers and, eventually, was caught. Committed to the Colorado State Reformatory, he escaped three times; each escape was followed by a string of robberies. During a stint in Multnomah County Jail in Portland, Oregon, he met Arnold Kyle, and the two paired up. Both were paroled from the county jail around the same time, and it wasn't long before they were back at their criminal ways; arrested for burglary, they were sentenced to Preston Reformatory Industrial School in Ione, California. Once again, they were released about the same time and made their way to Pittsburg, California, where they stayed with Kyle's sister Edna (AKA Kay Stone Wallace), who ran a brothel. The men became brothers-in-law when

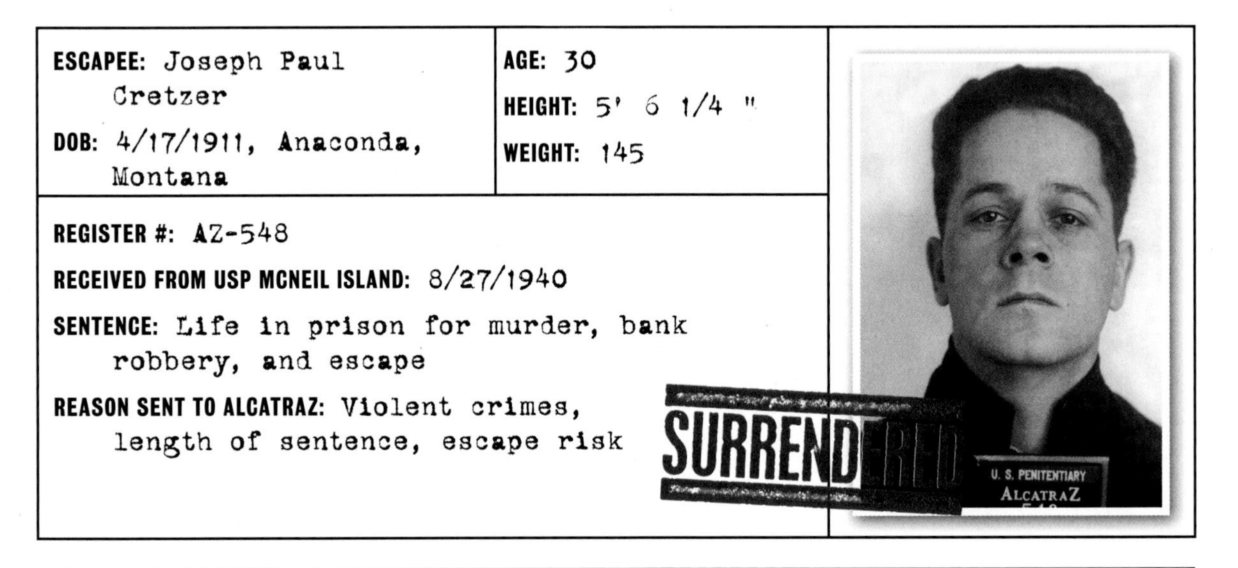
ESCAPEE: Joseph Paul Cretzer

DOB: 4/17/1911, Anaconda, Montana

AGE: 30

HEIGHT: 5' 6 1/4 "

WEIGHT: 145

REGISTER #: AZ-548

RECEIVED FROM USP MCNEIL ISLAND: 8/27/1940

SENTENCE: Life in prison for murder, bank robbery, and escape

REASON SENT TO ALCATRAZ: Violent crimes, length of sentence, escape risk

Record Form No. 8
(July, 1936)

CONDUCT RECORD

DEPARTMENT OF JUSTICE
PENAL AND CORRECTIONAL INSTITUTIONS

U. S. PENITENTIARY (Institution) ALCATRAZ, CALIFORNIA (Location)

Record of BARKDOLL, Lloyd H. No. 423-AZ

FPI INC—FLK—2-26-38—20000—11243-22

DATE	PRISON VIOLATIONS	DAYS LOST
3-22-40	CREATING DISTURBANCE IN CELL HOUSE. The above-named inmate was singing "Under The Sour Apple Tree" in a loud tone of voice between 6:30 and 6:00 P.M. today. Report #1278 by P.E. Tye, Jr. Officer. **ACTION: Stated he made some noise. To be placed in solitary confinement on restricted diet and to forfeit all privileges until further orders. E. J. Miller, Associate Warden.**	
3-24-40	Removed to regular cell and work assignment.	
7-9-40	CAUSING DISTURBANCE IN CELL HOUSE: While working on the 4 to 12 watch in the West Gallery this evening, there was considerable noise and hollering going on between "B" and "C" cell Blocks. While trying to locate it , I happened to be standing in a position where I had a good view of Cell #321 when the inmate opened up with a good blast about eight o'clock in the evening. Report by J.N.Jepson J.O. **ACTION: Stated he did not believe he hollered but the officer must be right. To forfeit all privileges for one week. E.J.Miller, Associate Warden**	
2-25-41	CAUSING DISTURBANCE IN CELL HOUSE. At about 5:15 P.M. and again at 7:15 P.M. this date. Barkdoll #423-AZ threw his effects from his cell and attempted to pry the door of his cell open with his iron bunk, destroying the bunk in the attempt. Report:- #350 by H. W. Weinhold, Lieut. **ACTION: Stated he had "Just bowed my neck, lost my head and raised hell". To be placed in open solitary on restricted diet and to forfeit all privileges until further orders. E. J. Miller, Associate Warden.**	
3-14-41	Removed to isolation cell.	
4-7-41	Removed to regular cell and work assignment, all priv. restored	
5-21-41	ATTEMPTED ESCAPE, ASSAULTING AN OFFICER, DESTRUCTION OF GOVERNMENT PROPERTY. On this date this inmate requested that I examine the cutting machine he was operating in the cutting room in the mat shop. As I stepped through the door he gave me a violent shove causing me to fall over #547-Kyle or #548-Cretzer. He then assisted in tying me up and attempted to escape by cutting a bar in thewindow and removing four panels of the detention sash. Report #138953 by C.E. Stoops, Jr. Officer. **ACTION: When interviewed in connection with the baove report, Bardoll stated that he wanted to go home and thought he had a chance but things didn't work out right." When questioned as to where he was going after he got out the window, if he did, he stated, "I'm not talking. He would make no further statement except that Number 462, Sam Shockley, wasn't in on this and was getting a 'bum-rap" addigg "we tied this son-of-a-bitch up also." Placed in solitary confinement on restricted diet and to forfeit all privileges until further orders. Recommend this man be placed in permanent segregation. E. J. Miller, Associate Warden**	
6-7-41	Removed to isolation "B" Block.	

7-27 & 28, 1941...CREATING DISTURBANCE IN CELL HOUSE. This inmate created disturbance in the cellhouse tonight. He was noisy from 5:30 till midnight. I warned him to be quiet at 10:45 and 11:45; while I was standing on "A" Block gallery he farted and whistled at me. There was a lot of yelling from this corner all night. Also, a lot of trash, bottles etc., were thrown on the floor. Report by H. Winegar, Jr. Officer.

(2)This inmate was whistling, shouting, and throwing out his personal belongings up until 1:00 A.M. this morning. Asked the reason he said that he was tired of being locked up, things were closing in on him, and he might as well keep everybody awake. After reasoning with him he was quiet from 1:15 and after. Report by Jepson, Jr. Officer. ACTION: Placed in solitary confinement, restricted diet, forfeit privileges until further notice. Barkdoll stated he just thought he would have some fun; the cell was so confining he just had to burst out with some noise. He siad that he expected to be punished for acting like a child and that he just didn't know why he had acted that way. E.J. Miller, Associate Warden.

8-9-41 Removed to isolation "B" Block.

8-27-41 CREATING DISTURBAnce in the cell house.

(1)Disorderly conduct, cursing, littering up the place, setting fires, creating disturbance, agitating; also throwing water at officer and rattled cup on bars. Report by Qesnell.

(2)This inmate after having set fires which were extinguished by Mr. Quessnell, shouted in a loud voice that I directed Mr. Quesnell to put the extinguisher on them. He also threatened to beat me or Mr. Quesnell up at the first opportunity. His raving kept the cellhouse in an uproar. Report by Acting Lieut. Prindle.
ACTION: Stated that the officer was a damned liar but finally stated that after it started that they might as well raise a lot of hell ehile they were at it. Placed in solitary confinement on restricted diet and to forfeit all privileges until further orders. E.J.Miller, Associate

9-10-41....... Removed to isolation "D" Block.

9-20-42 Removed from Isolation "D" Block, to regular cell, regular diet, regular work assignment(laundry). Privileges restored.A.W.

1-15-43 REFUSING TO WORK AND INSOLENCE: This man put in a request for a work change, from laundry to kitchen. When the Industrial Board turned down his request, stated he was not going to work and did not give a damm if he could not work in kitchen, baker shop, he would not work anywhere Report by E. J. Miller, Assoc. Warden No. 131864. ACTION: Solitary confinement, restricted diet, forf it all privileges until further orders. E. J. Miller, Assoc. Warden

1-26-43 Removed from solitary to regular isolation cell in "D" block Privileges remain forfeited.

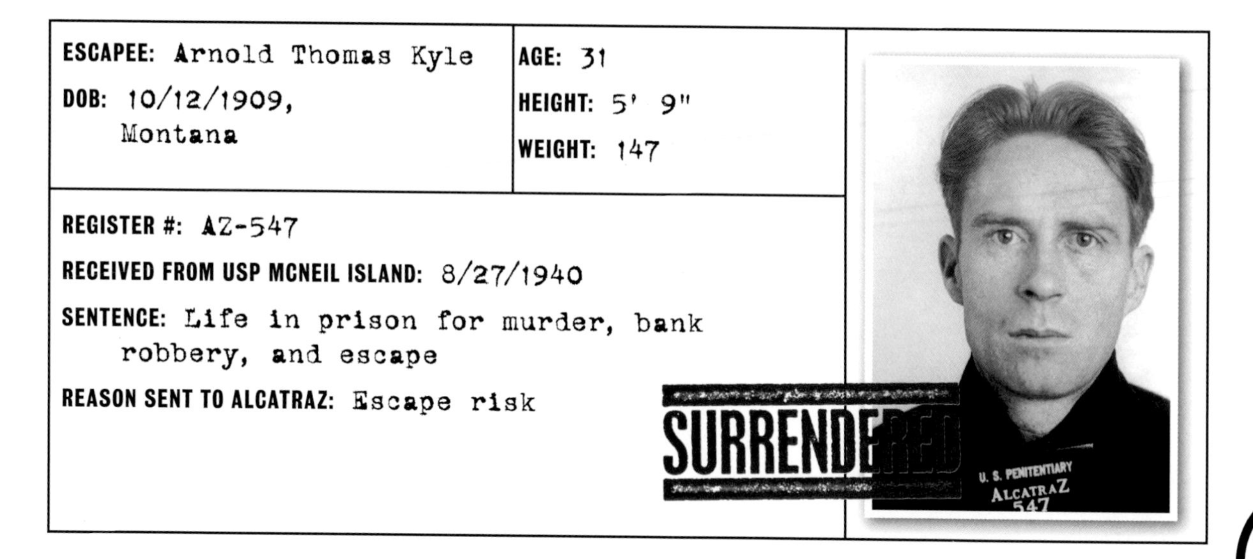
ESCAPEE: Arnold Thomas Kyle

AGE: 31

DOB: 10/12/1909, Montana

HEIGHT: 5' 9"

WEIGHT: 147

REGISTER #: AZ-547

RECEIVED FROM USP MCNEIL ISLAND: 8/27/1940

SENTENCE: Life in prison for murder, bank robbery, and escape

REASON SENT TO ALCATRAZ: Escape risk

Cretzer and Edna married in 1930; Kyle later married Cretzer's sister, Thelma. With Edna behind the wheel of a getaway car, they successfully robbed banks up and down the West Coast, hitting almost eighty over a period of eight months.

By September 1939, Cretzer was No. 4 on the FBI's most wanted list, and the pressure was on to capture him. Cretzer, Edna, and Kyle fled to Chicago, where Cretzer was captured and sentenced to twenty-five years in prison. He began serving his sentence at McNeil Island in February 1940. Two months later, he and Kyle escaped in a hijacked truck, but were recaptured after three days, and Cretzer had another five years tacked on to his sentence. While still in the Tacoma, Washington, courthouse, Cretzer again tried to escape, attacking a U.S. Marshal who subsequently died of a heart attack. This time when Cretzer was recaptured, he was charged with and convicted of murder. He arrived at Alcatraz in August 1940, handcuffed and leg-ironed to Arnold Kyle. Aggressive and shrewd, Cretzer intimidated the other cons and was soon viewed as a "boss" among the Alcatraz inmates.

Arnold Kyle's life mirrored Cretzer's in many ways. Born in Montana, Kyle was raised on his grandparents' farm, and later, by his father and stepmother in Portland, Oregon. He and his stepmother didn't get along, and Kyle was boarded out until he was eleven, then rejoined his father, who took him to a logging camp in Montana. He began stealing and as a result, spent time in the Montana State Industrial School. At age twenty-two, he was committed to the California state prison at San Quentin in Marin County (ironically, just a few miles by water from Alcatraz) after being convicted of a string of burglaries. He teamed up with Cretzer in Oregon, and the pair of bank robbers operated throughout California, Oregon, and Washington. Though he went to Chicago with his sister and

ESCAPEE: Sam Richard Shockley* **DOB:** 1/12/1909, Idabel, Oklahoma	**AGE:** 32 **HEIGHT:** 5' 8" **WEIGHT:** 142	SURRENDERED ALCATRAZ 462
REGISTER #: AZ-462 **RECEIVED FROM USP LEAVENWORTH:** 9/23/1938 **SENTENCE:** Life in prison for bank robbery and kidnapping **REASON SENT TO ALCATRAZ:** Long sentence, history of escape, dangerous, unable to adjust at Leavenworth		

* Who exactly took part in this attempt is in some dispute. In his book, *Alcatraz: The Gangster Years*, David Ward says that, despite the fact that Warden Johnston included Sam Shockley on the list of inmates involved in the escape attempt, Shockley actually played no part in it. Rather, Floyd Hamilton was both the plot's mastermind and leader, and in the aftermath, was able to avoid being named (and thus, punished). Ward also notes that every published account of this escape follows Warden Johnston's identification of the escapees, which includes Shockley and makes no mention of Hamilton. (See Escape File 7 for background on Hamilton.) As this account comes from the official record, it too includes Shockley as one of the players.

Cretzer, he didn't stay. Kyle was finally captured in Kansas, and in February 1940, along with Cretzer, was convicted of bank robbery and sentenced to twenty-five years in federal prison; both were sent to McNeil Island. In August 1940, Kyle and Cretzer arrived on the Rock in chains. Together, they continued to compile a notorious record of misconduct and attempted escape.

The sixth of seven children, **Sam Shockley** (AKA "Crazy Sam") quit school when he was twelve and went to work on the family farm. Gambling and thievery appealed to him more than farm work, however, and not long after he left home at eighteen, he was committed to a reformatory for stealing. Documents show he received two major head injuries while incarcerated. Following his release, he led a transient, unstable life. In 1938, he and Edward Johnson stole a shotgun and car, robbed a bank in Paoli, Oklahoma, and took several

A WARNING

In a memo dated June 12, 1945, from W.T. Hammack, Assistant Director, Bureau of Prisons to BOP Director James V. Bennett, Hammack observed:

> The Warden has made one departure from the policy established at the time the institution was taken over by us which creates a very dangerous hazard. Instead of keeping the prisoners in the area intended for their confinement and not allowing them on other parts of the island, he has (1) taken them into his own home as servants, (2) used them on the docks, and (3) used them as a clean-up squad about the Island. That makes it possible for the inmates to "case" the institution and know about everything on the Island. The men who are used outside the enclosure are just as clever as any of us and it goes without saying that they pass this information on to the rest of the inmates.
>
> Some time, some day, there will be a serious outbreak which will be possible because it is planned with full knowledge of all the Island protective devices, including the routine involving use and storage of the launch and custodial routine in the prison areas.

employees hostage. The hostages escaped, and Shockley was apprehended at his brother's home ten days later. He was tried, convicted, and sentenced to serve the remainder of his natural life in a federal penitentiary. After he arrived at Leavenworth on June 2, 1938, Shockley was examined by prison psychiatrists, who found him to be of well below normal intelligence, suffering from hallucinations, and prone to violent rages, which ultimately got him transferred to Alcatraz. Unfortunately, the Rock's strict routine had little effect; he remained uncontrollable and spent much of his time locked in isolation.

The Plan

Cretzer, Kyle, Barkdoll, and Shockley were assigned to work in the mat shop in the Model Industries Building at the northwest end of the island. With Barkdoll in the lead, the men devised a simple escape plan: outsmart and overpower the guard, use an electric emery wheel* to cut the window bars, scale

---

* In *Alcatraz: The Gangster Years*, David Ward says that the inmates bribed a prison employee to purchase and deliver a special cutting wheel, as they knew an emery wheel wouldn't be able to cut through the bars.

the fence, and make a quick run to the rocky shoreline and down to the water, where Edna Cretzer would be waiting in a high-powered getaway motorboat that would carry them all to freedom.

An inmate at work in the mat shop.

The Escape

Returning to the mat shop after the lunch break, Barkdoll lured Guard Clyde Stoops into one of the shop's side rooms by telling him a machine was out of order. Cretzer, Kyle, and Shockley were waiting, and pounced on Stoops, bound him hand and foot with heavy twine, stuffed a handkerchief in his mouth, and dragged him into a corner. They then herded the eight other convicts working in the shop into a separate room and went to work on the window, using a piece of pipe to pry off the reinforced inside casement, while Barkdoll took lookout duty.

The Model Industries Building

A WEAK LINK IN ALCATRAZ SECURITY

According to the Bureau of Prisons, federal prison industries were (and still are) intended to "contribute to the safety and security of Bureau facilities by keeping inmates constructively occupied." On Alcatraz, prison industries shops were originally housed in the Model Industries Building, a holdover from the island's military era (1850–1934).

From an inmate's point of view, this building's location directly above the waterline on the island's northwestern tip made it the most logical place from which to escape; four of the first seven getaway attempts originated here. Not only did the various shops—rubber mat, tailor, shoe, and woodworking among them—provide access to useful tools, the shoreline was relatively easy for the daring and the desperate to get to, and guards were unable to observe activity on the water-side of the building.

The New Industries Building—set far enough back from the island's edge for guards to have clear sightlines—was completed in 1940, and over time, all the prison industries shops were transferred to it. The Model Industries Building ended its prison days as a storage facility.

They were still working on the casement thirty minutes later when Barkdoll announced that C. J. Manning, superintendent of Industries, was headed to the shop. When Manning entered, he was grabbed, tied up, and hustled into the room with Stoops. The men finally got the casement pried off, then started on the toolproof bars with a small motor-driven emery stone. Next, Lionel Johnson, the work area yard supervisor, was spotted approaching the shop. Once inside, he got the same treatment as Stoops and Manning. Not long after, Paul Madigan, captain of the guards, was added to the group of bound and gagged officers. By this time, the convicts were desperate. It was 3:30 and they'd been working frantically since 1; they needed to cut through at least two—or if possible, three—steel bars to make an opening large enough for them to get through, and they were still working on their first bar with the clearly useless emery wheel.

The gang was becoming increasingly discouraged. Madigan managed to work his gag loose, and then quietly spoke to the men. "Boys, it's just about time for the officers here to report to the Armorer, and if they don't, you're going to have a flock of officers storming in with machine guns. So you might as well give yourselves up before this goes too far."

Barkdoll looked at Kyle and Kyle looked at Cretzer, who was staring bitterly at the empty channel, then at the undamaged window bars. "Joe, we're getting deader every minute," said Kyle. "We'll come up again, wait and see." Convinced at last that it just couldn't be done, Cretzer hurled the grinder against the shop wall and watched as Barkdoll freed their captives.

PAUL MADIGAN—COOL UNDER FIRE

Paul Madigan came up through the ranks at Alcatraz: guard, lieutenant, captain, associate warden, and finally warden. The diplomatic skills he exhibited in the 1941 escape attempt served him well throughout his long career. As warden from 1955 to 1961, he made an effort to meet the needs of prisoners and staff, but wasn't afraid to issue unpopular orders. The guards called him "Promising Paul," because he frequently made promises he didn't keep. Madigan, who was a devout Catholic, attended mass with the prisoners; did away with the solitary confinement diet of bread and water; and arranged for inmates to have special meals on holidays. During his tenure as warden, there were only two escape attempts (see Escape Files 11 and 12). In 1961, Madigan was transferred as warden to USP McNeil Island.

Administrative
Form No. 7
Rev. 2/27/40

REQUEST FOR RESTORATION OF GOOD TIME

Name of Prisoner Kyle, Arnold Thomas No. 547-AZ Institution Alcatraz

Date Received 6-17-39 (McN) Date sentence began June 7, 1939

Term 30 years and Life Conc. Fine { Committed / Not Committed } Costs { Committed / Not Committed }

Minimum expiration Life Maximum Life Eligible for parole 10-20-55

Total good time allowance 3600 on 30 yrs. --- Amount forfeited 1107 MB 395 Date 4-29-40

New date eligible for release Life Reasons for forfeiture:

Escaped from McNeil Island custody on 4-11-40 and recaptured on 4-14-40, in company with #547, Cretzer, another inmate at McNeil Island. (Note: While the forfeiture does not change concurrent life sentence, it clouds the entire sentence.)

Date paroled Date returned from parole

Date escaped 4-11-40 Sentence for escape 5 yrs. consec. Date 8-22-40 Court W-Wash. Tacoma

Date committed to institution after escape McNeil Island, then to Alcatraz, 8-27-40

Date August 16, 1957

To Director, Bureau of Prisons

I recommend that 400 days good time allowance

be restored to Arnold Thomas Kyle No. 547-AZ

Reasons therefore: This man has maintained a clear conduct record since January 1955 and his general attutude and adjustment have continued to improve. He is an excellant worker in the industries. Last year 300 days of his forfeited good time were restored and the Committee felt that he is deserving of the restoration of a substantial portion of the balance at this time.

Acting Warden J. B. Latimer
Institution Alcatraz

Date AUG 27 1957 The restoration of 400 days good time allowance is approved.

FOR THE ATTORNEY GENERAL

J. Bennett
Director

(Original. To be retained in the office of the Bureau of Prisons.)

Edna Cretzer had her own long rap sheet.

The Aftermath

The four men surrendered and were marched to solitary confinement. The daring escape plot, which had the makings of a slaughter, ended without a shot fired or a person harmed. Alcatraz officials later learned that Edna Cretzer, a major player in a statewide prostitution ring, had been picked up by San Francisco vice officers that same morning.

The foiled escape seemed to change Barkdoll, who become a model inmate—cheerful, friendly, and cooperative; he worked in the officers' dining room (to which only the most trusted inmates were assigned) and started an inmate orchestra, the Rock Islanders. In 1950, after suffering a massive heart attack, he died in the prison's hospital and his body was sent for burial to Coquille, Oregon. Kyle too settled down and made an effort to reduce his time through good behavior. On the other hand, Cretzer's five years on D Block did nothing to dampen his drive to escape. In May 1946, along with Shockley and four others, he took part in the violent siege known as the Battle of Alcatraz (see Escape File 10).

The *San Francisco Examiner* and *San Francisco Chronicle* covered the story in great detail. In a *Chronicle* interview, Warden Johnston observed that every man in the group would seize upon the slightest opportunity to make a break.

Escape 6

Icy Bay Waters Greet Crazy Con

Lone wolf dives into bay, headed for mainland.

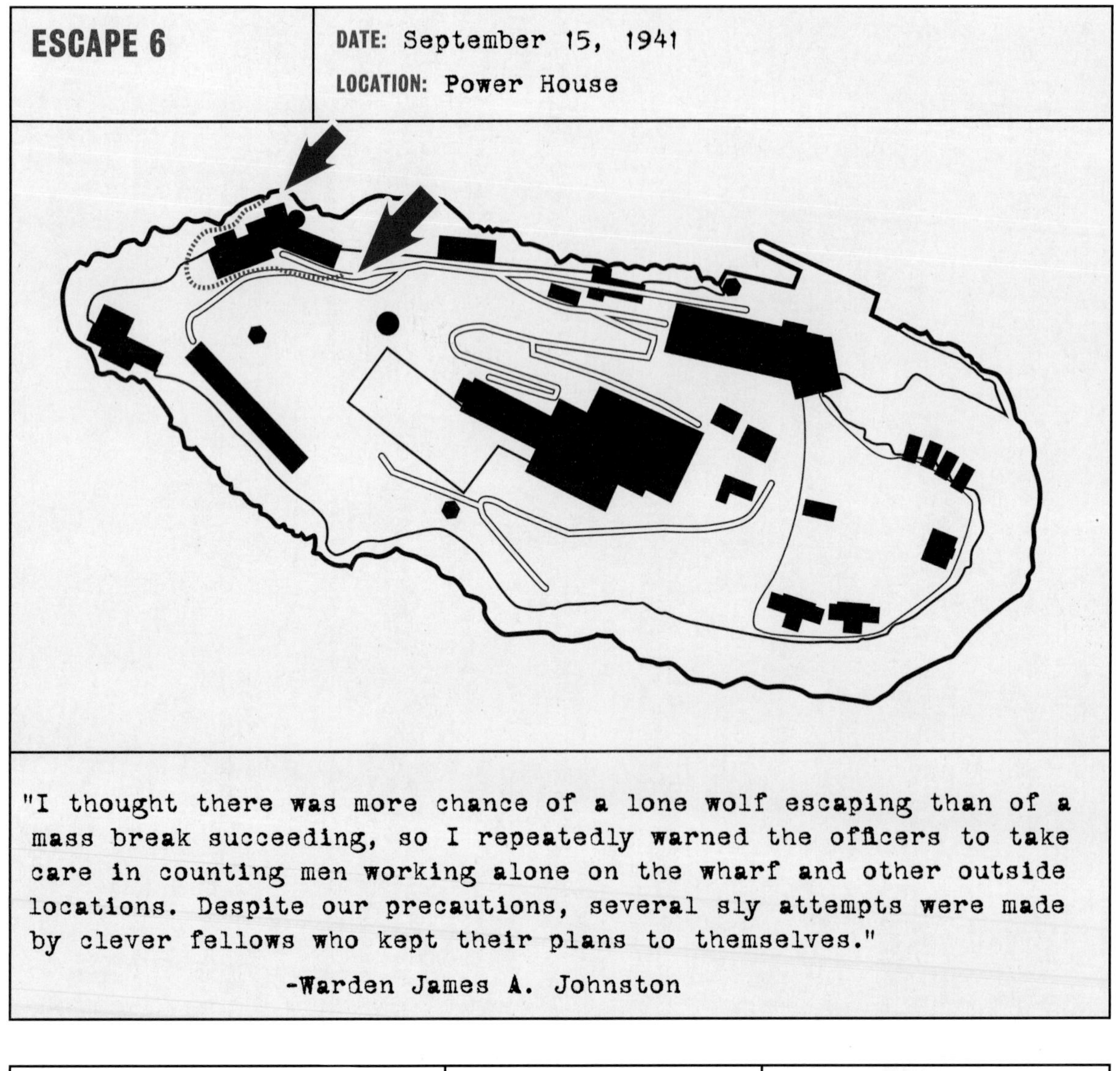

ESCAPE 6

DATE: September 15, 1941

LOCATION: Power House

"I thought there was more chance of a lone wolf escaping than of a mass break succeeding, so I repeatedly warned the officers to take care in counting men working alone on the wharf and other outside locations. Despite our precautions, several sly attempts were made by clever fellows who kept their plans to themselves."

-Warden James A. Johnston

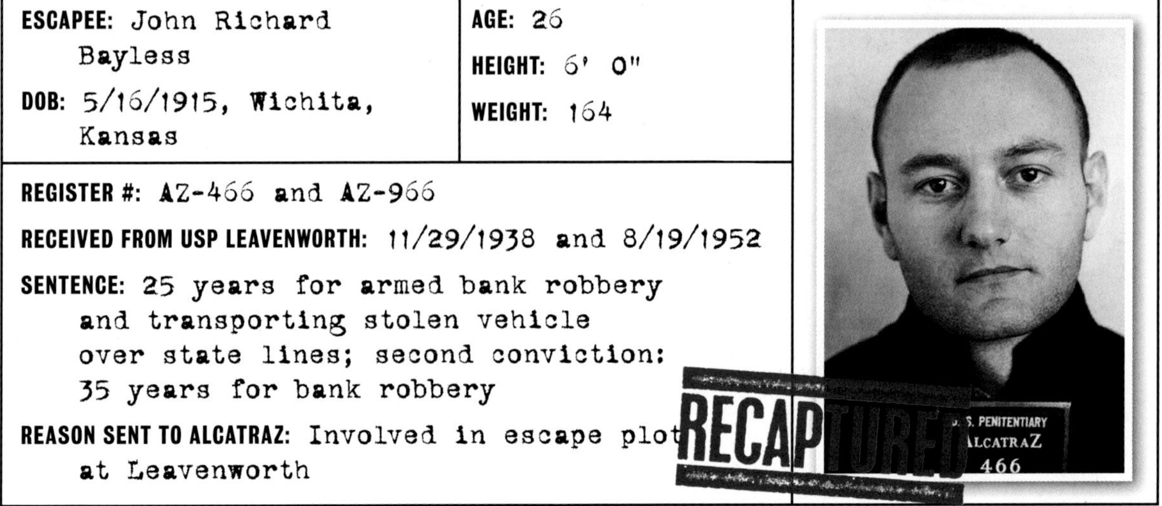

ESCAPEE: John Richard Bayless

DOB: 5/16/1915, Wichita, Kansas

AGE: 26

HEIGHT: 6' 0"

WEIGHT: 164

REGISTER #: AZ-466 and AZ-966

RECEIVED FROM USP LEAVENWORTH: 11/29/1938 and 8/19/1952

SENTENCE: 25 years for armed bank robbery and transporting stolen vehicle over state lines; second conviction: 35 years for bank robbery

REASON SENT TO ALCATRAZ: Involved in escape plot at Leavenworth

The year 1941 was the first in which two escapes were attempted. Just months after four convicts took correctional officers hostage, another inmate made a break for it. John Bayless, who was considered "low maintenance" by prison officials, saw a chance and took it while assigned to the garbage detail.

Road to Alcatraz

In the prison record books, **John Bayless** occupies a rare position as one of a handful of men consigned to Alcatraz twice. Born into a middle-class family, Bayless was the only child of a railroad worker and a homemaker. His first sixteen years were unremarkable; like many of his contemporaries, he was a Boy Scout, interested in science, and a regular church-goer.

When he was seventeen, his parents divorced and he went to live with his maternal grandmother and her daughter in Willow Springs, Missouri. He completed high school there in 1933, then entered the US Navy and trained as an aircraft mechanic in Long Beach, California. Military life didn't suit Bayless, however, and within a year, he began what would become a lifetime of crime by writing a bad check, using it to buy a Ford roadster, and going AWOL. Arrested as a deserter, he was dishonorably discharged, then convicted of forgery and interstate transportation of a stolen vehicle. In 1935, he began serving a two-year sentence in the federal reformatory in El Reno, Oklahoma, which apparently taught him nothing. Once released, he quickly returned to his criminal pursuits.

On November 2, 1937, Bayless and a partner, Orville Sims, robbed the Farmers and Merchants Bank at Mansfield, Missouri, of $606.51. Arrested and sentenced to twenty-five years in prison, Bayless arrived at Leavenworth on February 1, 1938. He refused to work, made threatening remarks, had a contraband

Their happy journey ended in a bank robbery

HONEYMOON

IT WAS October. The woods along the road between Strong City, Kansas, and Wichita, were aflame with color. With a feeling of luxury, Gwendolyn Bayless sat back in the car beside her young husband, John Richard, a good-looking boy of twenty-one. She had met him a month before in Kansas City, Missouri, her home town. It was a case of love at first sight. They were both so eager that no time was wasted on courtship. They were married almost immediately.

Gwendolyn was proud of her six-foot husband. He was so attentive and considerate; so much so that there was no doubt that his feelings for her were real. She had gathered that he came from a fine family, for he talked and dressed well, and this idea was substantiated by the stories he told her.

Their first two weeks of married life were uneventful. Her husband had furnished an apartment and the future seemed to offer nothing but happiness. There was one thing, however, that occasionally made her pout, though she said nothing. John would frequently absent himself for hours at a time, and give no explanation. One day, reading the questioning look in her eyes, he said:

"You wonder why I don't work, Gwen, don't you? Don't let that trouble you. There's a reason. I didn't want to tell you because I wanted it to be a surprise. Well, you get the surprise now. I have money coming from an inheritance. Next year we get it all."

What could Gwendolyn do but throw her arms around him and tell him she was more happy than ever?

The excitement of the quick succession of events that had come to her and changed her life so completely made the girl restless. She wanted to do something; to tell somebody all about her good fortune; her wonderful young husband. Finally she suggested that they take his car and drive to Wichita, Kansas, where her mother lived. It would make a little honeymoon trip, "and my mother will be glad to see me—and you, too," she finished shyly. John agreed at once. So, with another couple, both youngsters, they were now on their way.

It was October 29th, and hot. The sun seemed to have forgotten that November was just around the corner. It glared down brightly on the highway, and the heat was out of season for such an otherwise autumn-like day.

John, driving, commented on it.

"Why don't you take your coat off?" suggested Gwendolyn.

The youthful bridegroom thought it a good idea. He placed it on the car seat beside his wife. Accidentally she touched it. There was something hard in the pocket. Running her hand down into it,

Mrs. Bayless started her marriage in a hospital bed . . .

she felt an object that had the hard smoothness of metal. Its shape soon told her what she had discovered.

"Why, John," she exclaimed, and there was a tinge of alarm in her voice, "it's a gun! What are you doing with it?"

He laughed good-humoredly. "Sure it's a gun," he said. "How did you guess it? When we get to Wichita, my pal and I are going hunting rabbits, aren't we?" and he called to his seventeen-year-old friend in the back seat, while he laughed again his youthful, musical laugh she liked to hear.

"What a swell idea!" she exclaimed. Her knowledge of guns was not extensive, hence the idea of using a revolver to shoot rabbits did not occur to her as a new and strange departure in the sport of hunting.

They drove through Cottonwood Falls, Bayless still complaining of the heat. When the other young man offered to take the wheel and give him a rest, he was glad to relinquish it.

But with the exchange of drivers, things began to happen. Speeding up the car with the energy and enthusiasm of an untired mind and arms, the youngster soon had it careening along at so fast a clip that both girls uttered exclamations of dismay. He was laughing at their fears when suddenly the sedan leaped over the shoulder of the road, overturned several times and then plunged into a ditch.

HOLDUP

by

Captain L. E. BOWERY

WICHITA, KANSAS, POLICE DEPARTMENT

with PLINY CASTANIEN

Fortunately it came to a stop right side up, and the driver and his companion escaped with scarcely a scratch. But John and Gwendolyn, who had been riding in the back seat, were pinned beneath the wreckage. John was able to extricate himself, but his wife was apparently seriously hurt. She complained of an excruciating pain in her back, and one of her legs hurt her terribly. They finally managed to drag her out.

Young Bayless was alarmed for his bride. He had torn his hand and a wrenched back kept him from standing up straight, but he would think of nothing except getting immediate aid for Gwendolyn. A doctor was quickly summoned. A brief examination and he pronounced the girl's injuries serious. They must get her to a hospital as soon as possible, for her life might be in danger. Then more bad news. The nearest hospital was in Wichita, more than 100 miles away. This did not deter the alarmed Bayless. With the physician's assistance they obtained an ambulance and the whole party, with Gwendolyn on a stretcher, sped to Wichita, leaving the wrecked car to be towed to a garage in Cottonwood Falls.

An examination at St. Francis Hospital showed that the girl was suffering from a broken vertebra in the neck and a broken leg. Her young husband gripped his hands fiercely at the sight of the agony in her face. There was no immediate danger, the doctor said, but she would have to remain there for weeks.

John was torn with grief and worry. He had no money and none of the party had any. He hated to leave her, but finally had to, telling her that he would notify her mother of the accident.

♦ Orletta Sims knew nothing of the crooked activities of her husband

knife, and got involved in an escape plot, all of which earned him his first ticket to Alcatraz. The habitual criminal would return in 1952 to serve thirty-five years for murder.

The Plan

Much like Joseph Bowers (Escape File 1), Bayless appears to have acted spontaneously. It seems most likely that, when a dense fog drifted over the island, he saw his chance and made his way from his outdoor work detail to the water. He was without tools and later admitted that he had "ribbed" himself into believing he could make it to the mainland.

The Escape

Bayless was assigned to the garbage detail, which most inmates considered a choice job because it allowed them to work all over the island with limited supervision. At about 3:45 PM on September 15, just before the inmates were rounded up for the final count and returned to the cellhouse, Bayless slipped away and dropped to the rocky shore near the power house, where he stripped down to his underwear and eased into the water. The shock he got from the cold water quickly changed his mind.

Within minutes, the guards noticed that Bayless was missing and notified the Control Center, which sounded the alarm. Junior Officer Wilkinson heard a splash, spotted Bayless in the water, and ordered him to return to shore. Bayless obeyed, shivering and defeated. Taken to the hospital for examination, Bayless was bruised, battered, and sick from swallowing salt water, according to the doctor's report.

Power house and Quartermaster building (foreground).

The Aftermath

Bayless went from the prison hospital to isolation. His diet was restricted and all privileges were forfeited, as were 3,000 days of statutory good time that he had built up since his arrival on the island.

Two months later, when taken to San Francisco to appeal a robbery indictment, Bayless tried to bolt from the courtroom; as he dashed to the side door, he grappled with the bailiff and was floored by a punch in the jaw from a deputy marshal. Taken back to Alcatraz, he was once again tossed in isolation and received an additional five years in prison for his trouble.

Surprisingly, Bayless' days as a bank robber and escape artist were far from over. Transferred to Leavenworth in 1950, he was paroled in 1951, robbed another bank, and was back in jail in 1952. Convicted and sentenced to serve thirty years, he began a second stint on Alcatraz on August 19, 1952, and was among the last prisoners transferred off the island when the prison was closed in 1963. Sent to McNeil Island, Bayless made a successful escape; when he was finally recaptured, he was sentenced to forty-five years. Paroled again, he attempted to rob yet another bank and was sent back to Leavenworth.

A LIFE BEHIND BARS

Bayless lived in a penitentiary setting for the majority of his adult life, and, according to a report by Leavenworth staff, gave every indication of being willing "to live in this environment for quite some time into the future. He has no contact with any family members . . . and does not appear to be able to function in the community." Inside the prison walls, he was deemed friendly and hardworking. He liked to play bridge and chess, and learned to play the trombone while at Alcatraz. An avid sports fan, he also played softball and handball.

One of his few requests, made in 1954, was that the inmates be allowed to listen to the World Series broadcasts. He read one or two books a week and subscribed to *Bridge World*, *Sports Illustrated*, *Sports Afield*, *Sporting News*, *Popular Mechanics*, and *Alaskan Sports*. Despite his pleasant demeanor, in a 1955 review, Alcatraz officials noted that "he is still to be regarded as desperate and would likely sneak away if the opportunity presented itself."

Escape 7

Texas Gangster Leads Bust-Out

Karpis mobster recaptured-former Public Enemy eludes guards.

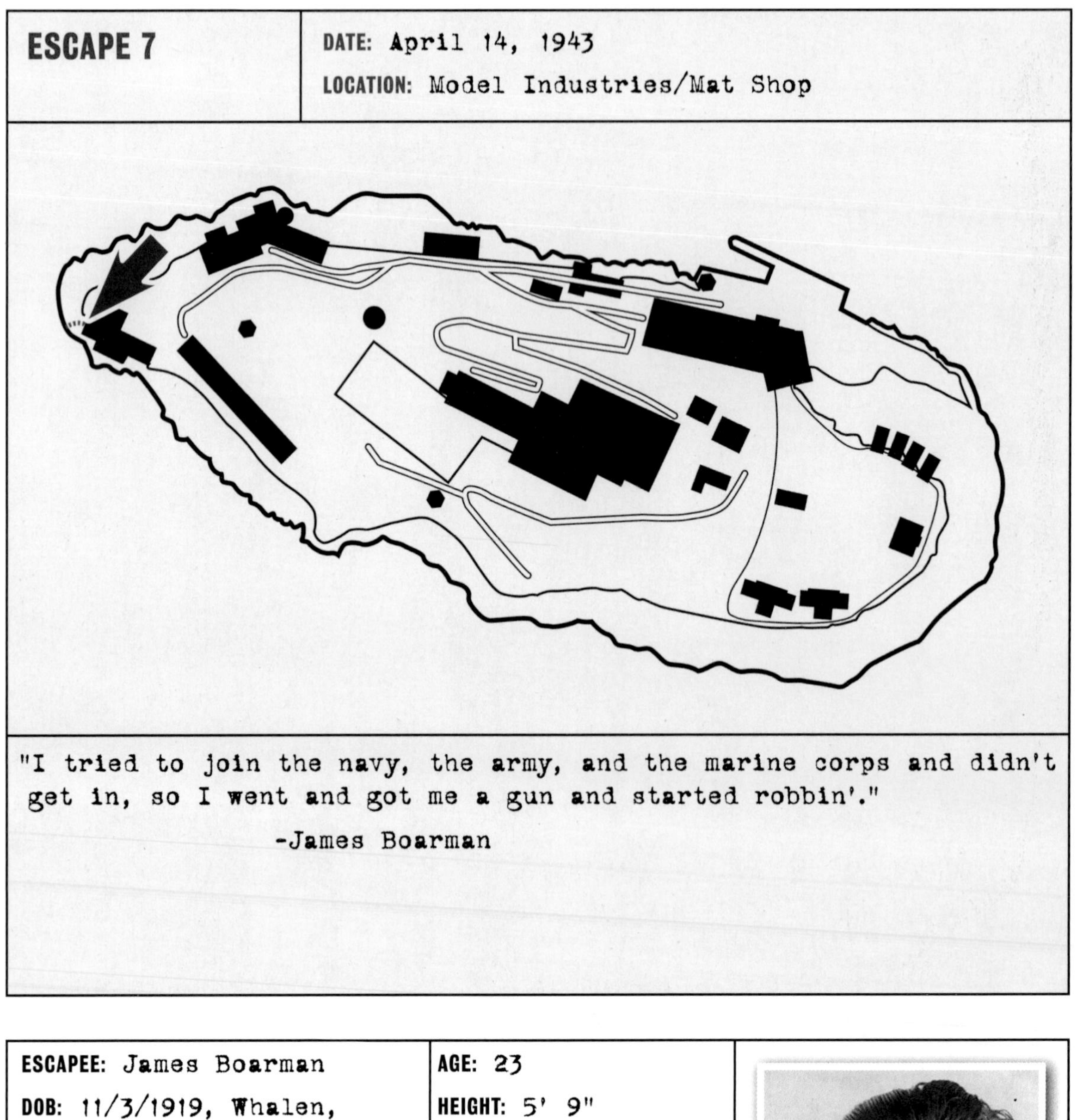

ESCAPE 7

DATE: April 14, 1943

LOCATION: Model Industries/Mat Shop

"I tried to join the navy, the army, and the marine corps and didn't get in, so I went and got me a gun and started robbin'."

-James Boarman

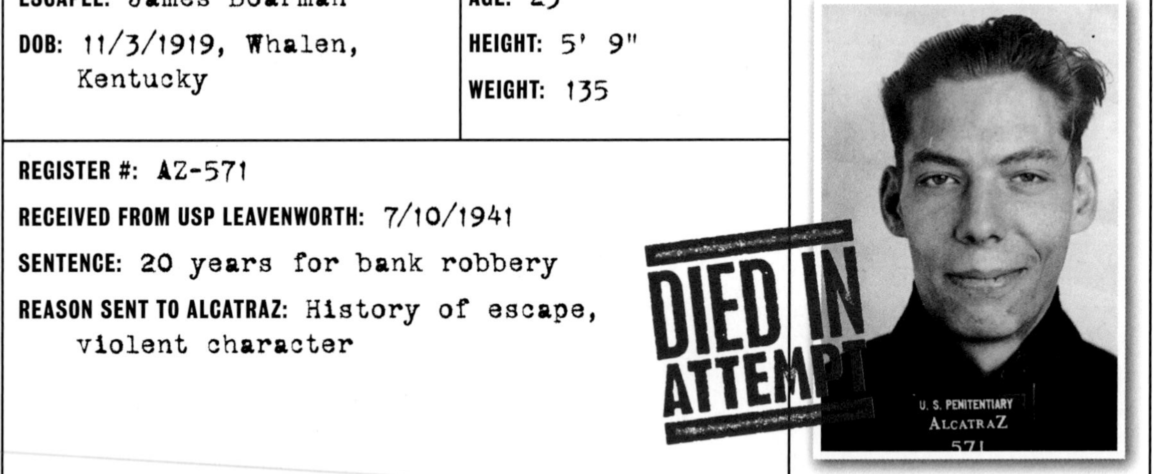

ESCAPEE: James Boarman

DOB: 11/3/1919, Whalen, Kentucky

AGE: 23

HEIGHT: 5' 9"

WEIGHT: 135

REGISTER #: AZ-571

RECEIVED FROM USP LEAVENWORTH: 7/10/1941

SENTENCE: 20 years for bank robbery

REASON SENT TO ALCATRAZ: History of escape, violent character

Being behind bars didn't stop Floyd Hamilton—friend of Bonnie and Clyde and one of the country's deadliest public enemies—from scouting for a crew and hatching a scheme to bust out of the Rock. Joining him were other underworld criminals whose names had also made headlines across the nation.

ESCAPE FILE 7

Road to Alcatraz

James Boarman found trouble early on. After his father's death, his mother relocated the family—which included eight children—from Kentucky to Indiana. At seventeen, he stole his first car. Out on probation, he went on stealing cars, a habit that eventually landed him in the federal reformatory at El Reno, Oklahoma. After a botched escape attempt, he was transferred to USP Lewisburg, from which he was released in 1939. In an attempt to go straight, he worked at RCA Radio Company for a short time before being laid off and returning to a life of crime. "I got me a job and did go straight," Boarman said. "I lost that job, and couldn't find another one for hell." His crime spree ended with armed bank robbery, and his dangerous nature earned him a transfer from Leavenworth to Alcatraz.

Harold Brest was a handsome, cold-blooded criminal first sent to prison for blackmail when he was nineteen. After his mother died, his father raised him, along with five other children. Completing seventh grade at age fifteen, Brest dropped out of school and began his criminal career. Starting out with trespassing, Brest quickly progressed to auto theft, blackmail, kidnapping, bank robbery, and violation of the Dyer Act; he once claimed that he had robbed so many drug stores, filling stations, and the like that he couldn't remember them all. Always armed, he said he would shoot any police officer who attempted to

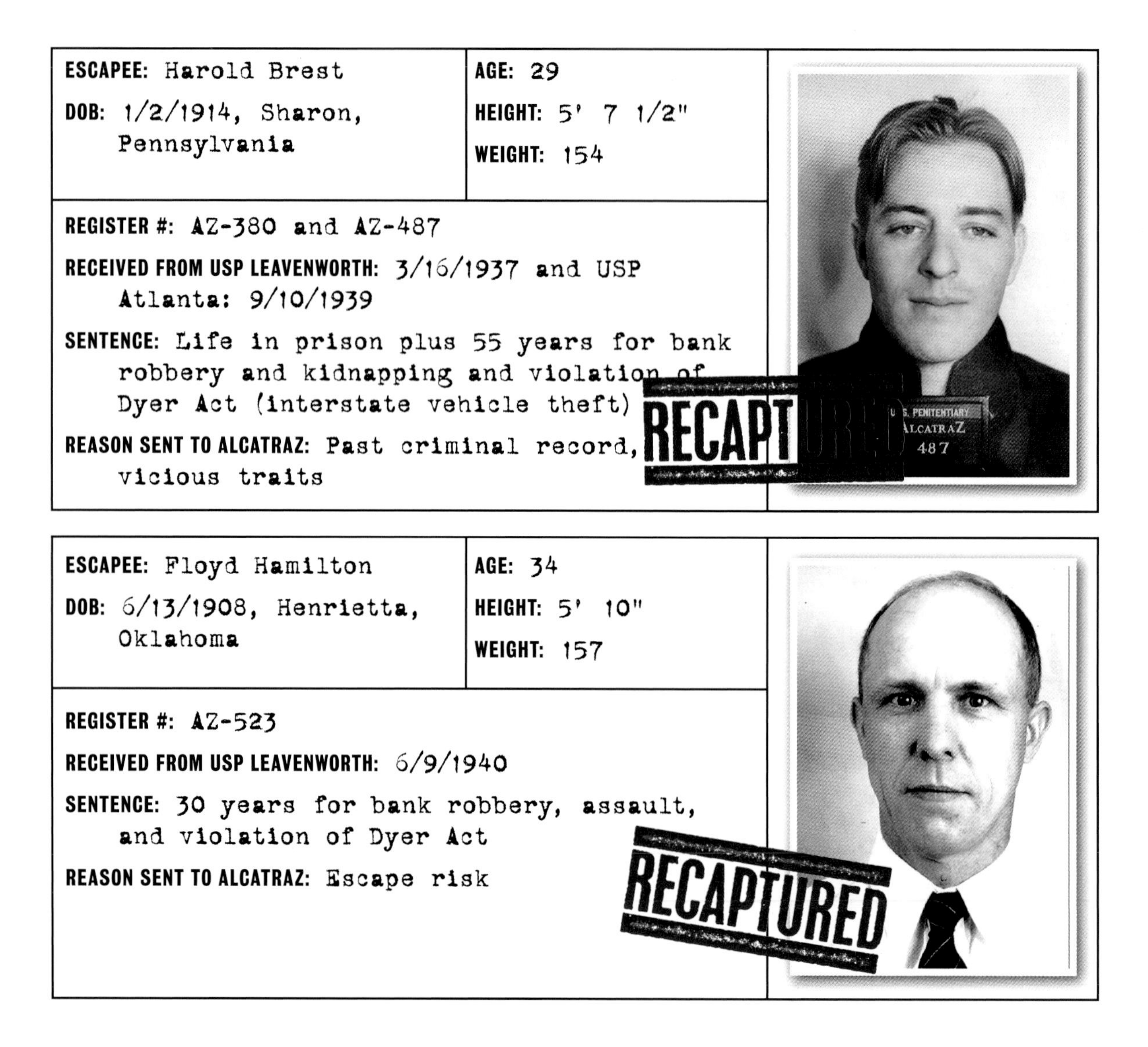
ESCAPEE: Harold Brest
DOB: 1/2/1914, Sharon, Pennsylvania
AGE: 29
HEIGHT: 5' 7 1/2"
WEIGHT: 154
REGISTER #: AZ-380 and AZ-487
RECEIVED FROM USP LEAVENWORTH: 3/16/1937 and USP Atlanta: 9/10/1939
SENTENCE: Life in prison plus 55 years for bank robbery and kidnapping and violation of Dyer Act (interstate vehicle theft)
REASON SENT TO ALCATRAZ: Past criminal record, vicious traits

ESCAPEE: Floyd Hamilton
DOB: 6/13/1908, Henrietta, Oklahoma
AGE: 34
HEIGHT: 5' 10"
WEIGHT: 157
REGISTER #: AZ-523
RECEIVED FROM USP LEAVENWORTH: 6/9/1940
SENTENCE: 30 years for bank robbery, assault, and violation of Dyer Act
REASON SENT TO ALCATRAZ: Escape risk

capture him, and expressed regret that the shooting of one policeman didn't end in death. Brest—like John Bayless (see Escape File 6)—also had the distinction of being one of the few convicts sent to Alcatraz twice. During his first stay on the island, he won his way out on a writ of habeas corpus on the grounds that he had been deprived of counsel when convicted of bank robbery in 1937. Unfortunately for Brest, as soon as he got out, he was rearrested, retried, and sentenced to life plus fifty-five years, a much stiffer sentence than his original twenty-five-year term.

Floyd Hamilton went from an uneventful youth to become one of the FBI's most wanted criminals of the 1930s. The second in a family of six children, he was raised in Dallas, Texas; attended church; married at the age of nineteen; and took at job at an oil refinery. But when the plant closed and he was unable to find work, Hamilton became a bank robber. He had a youthful association with the notorious Bonnie Parker and Clyde Barrow before the two were shot to death in 1934, and in 1938, he teamed up with Ted Walters (who would also attempt to escape from Alcatraz; see Escape File 8). Arrested after a daring holdup in the office of a Coca-Cola bottling plant, Hamilton served time at Leavenworth, was implicated in an escape plot there, and sent to Alcatraz. (Hamilton's brother, Raymond, was executed in 1935 for the murder of a guard during a break from a Texas state prison.)

Fred Hunter completed eighth grade and went to work as a mechanic and welder, but soon traded steady employment for a career as a gambler. Through this activity, he became acquainted with Alvin "Old Creepy" Karpis and his gang, and was involved in a string of crimes, including mail robbery and assault in Ohio. In 1936, he was convicted of harboring Karpis in Louisiana and in 1937, was sentenced to twenty-five years in federal prison for mail robbery. Described by Alcatraz physicians as undersized and poorly nourished, he suffered over the years from a variety of medical ailments, including tuberculosis, chronic sinusitis, and Dupuytren's contracture (which affects the connective tissue under the skin of the palm and eventually pulls fingers into a permanently bent position) of both hands. In 1948, he pleaded for a transfer to MCFP Springfield, Missouri, for treatment of his hands and to get away from the damp climate, which affected his health. Given his weak physical condition, it's questionable as to how far he intended to go with the escape plot.

ESCAPE FILE 7

ESCAPEE: Fred Hunter

DOB: 10/13/1899, Warren, Ohio

AGE: 43

HEIGHT: 5' 7 1/2"

WEIGHT: 129

REGISTER #: AZ-402

RECEIVED FROM USP LEAVENWORTH: 7/6/37

SENTENCE: 25 years, 10 months and 9 days for postal robbery, assault, conspiracy, harboring a fugitive

REASON SENT TO ALCATRAZ: Long sentence, prior association with "big-time" gangsters

RECAPTURED

Administrative Form No. 66
November 1938

DEPARTMENT OF JUSTICE

WASHINGTON

July 7, 1941

To the Warden, U. S. Penitentiary, Leavenworth, Kansas

WHEREAS, in accordance with the authority contained in title 18, sections 744b and 753f, U. S. Code, the Attorney General by the Director of the Bureau of Prisons has ordered the

transfer of James Arnold Boarman, #57662 #571 Az

from the U. S. Penitentiary, Leavenworth, Kansas

to the U. S. Penitentiary, Alcatraz Island, California

NOW THEREFORE, you, the above-named officer, are hereby authorized and directed to execute this order by causing the removal of said prisoner, together with the original writ of commitment and other official papers as above ordered and to incur the necessary expense and include it in your regular accounts.

And you, the warden, superintendent, or official in charge of the institution in which the prisoner is now confined, are hereby authorized to deliver the prisoner in accordance with the above order; and you, the warden, superintendent, or official in charge of the institution to which the transfer has been ordered, are hereby authorized and directed to receive the said prisoner into your custody and him to safely keep until the expiration of his sentence or until he is otherwise discharged according to law.

By direction of the Attorney General,

FRANK LOVELAND
Acting *Assistant Director, Bureau of Prisons.*

Safer custody - industries strike

ORIGINAL.—To be left at institution to which prisoner is transferred

U. S. GOVERNMENT PRINTING OFFICE 7—2158

The Plan

Hamilton incorporated elements of some of the past escape attempts into his plan, which involved an escape from the former mat shop, where the inmates now made cement blocks to weigh down the navy's submarine nets. Like Roe and Cole in 1937 (see Escape File 2), they stole pieces of army uniforms from the laundry and stuffed them into fuel containers; they marked the cans and placed them near similar canisters in a nearby storeroom. They were counting on the cans to keep them afloat in the cold, fast water surrounding the island. For months, they spent time secretly sawing through some of the shop's window bars, carefully concealing their work with grease and paint. All that remained was to wait for a dense fog to blanket the island—something that happened on a regular basis.

SAN FRANCISCO BAY: THE FINAL BARRIER TO FREEDOM

During the twenty-nine years Alcatraz was a federal prison, its inmates cut through tool-proof bars, climbed over barbed wire and chain-link fences, tied up unsuspecting guards, and slipped past armed men in watch towers. But the one-and-a-quarter-mile swim from the island to the San Francisco shoreline often ended their race to escape. Some who made it to the island's edge just gave up. Others, like Floyd Hamilton, entered the water, only to swim back minutes later. One, caught up in the bay's swift currents, was swept to shore near the Golden Gate, where he was quickly spotted and captured. Five disappeared into San Francisco Bay, never to be seen again. Could they have made the swim to freedom?

A lot of prisoners worried about "man-eating" sharks, and Alcatraz guards did little to calm their fears. In fact, the only sharks in the bay are small bottom-feeders. The obstacles posed by the bay were no myth, however: temperatures of 50 to 55 degrees Fahrenheit year-round, powerful tides, treacherous currents. Today, more than a thousand people of all ages swim from the island to San Francisco's waterfront every year. The "Escape from the Rock" triathlon features a one-and-a-half-mile swim, two-and-a-half-mile run, and thirteen-mile bike ride and draws athletes from around the world. The popular event is held when currents are at a low point, the well-conditioned swimmers wear wet suits, and there are plenty of rescue boats on hand. The cons on Alcatraz couldn't lift weights or eat special diets to get in shape, they couldn't take practice swims, and they didn't have access to the tide charts that might have given them a critical advantage in their escapes. So, for the many convicts who gazed across the bay and dreamed of freedom, the odds of making it were slim.

The Escape

At 10 AM on April 14, 1943, the men made their move. Brandishing prison-made knives, the four cons overpowered Officer George Smith, and swiftly gagged and bound him. Captain Henry Weinhold, a tough former Marine called "Bullethead" by the inmates, was making his morning rounds when he noticed that Smith was missing from his station. As he stepped in the doorway of the mat shop, Brest and Boarman seized him, bound his ankles and wrists, and stuffed a handkerchief in his mouth. Quickly stripping to their underwear, the four men smeared themselves with industrial grease for protection against the cold water, kicked out the pre-cut bars, and leaped through the window. In their haste, they left behind two of the four cans they had planned to use as floats when they proved too hard to pull through the window. Miraculously, the men plunged thirty feet down a sheer cliff to the rock-strewn shore without serious injury. Just as they entered the water, Captain Weinhold worked his gag loose and shouted for help, but the saw running in the woodshop drowned out his cries.

Smith was unable to remove his gag, but moved closer to Weinhold, who managed to blow Smith's whistle. Meanwhile, Frank Johnson, one of the tower guards, spotted the escapees in the water and opened fire. Within seconds, the alarm siren was sounded, the prison went into high alert, and inmates were rushed to their cells.

The Aftermath

The prison launch *McDowell* sped away from the dock; as it rounded the island, officers on board saw Brest, desperately clutching an unconscious Boarman. The water around the men was crimson—Brest had been shot in the arm and Boarman had taken a lethal bullet to the head. The launch pulled up alongside them, and as Brest reached up toward the guard, he let go of Boarman, who slipped beneath the surface. Brest was hauled stark naked out of the cold water and returned to the prison hospital. Boarman's body was never recovered.

Hunter, who had injured his back and cut his hands in his leap, gave up on swimming and took refuge in a nearby cave. Searching the shoreline, officers spotted blood at the entrance to the cave—as though someone had been leaning on the rocks for support. One of the guards ordered Hunter to come out. When he didn't respond, the guard fired a pistol shot. Stoop-shouldered, Hunter quickly appeared. After less than eight hours of liberty, he was returned to his cell. Before the escape, Hunter had been eligible for parole in two years, but after, his sentence was lengthened to fifteen years and he was slapped with a $15,000 fine.

For Immediate Release
TUESDAY, APRIL 13, 1943
(3:30 P.M.)

DEPARTMENT OF JUSTICE

Director James V. Bennett of the Federal Bureau of Prisons announced today that one of four prisoners who attempted to escape from Alcatraz at approximately 10:35 this morning by overpowering prison guards and jumping into San Francisco Bay has been recaptured and that the remaining three are believed to have been killed by gunfire or to have drowned.

The recaptured prisoner is Harold M. Brest, who was committed to Alcatraz on June 23, 1939, from Pittsburgh, Pa., to serve a life sentence for kidnaping and bank robbery.

The missing prisoners are:

James A. Boarman, serving 20 years for violation of the National Bank Robbery Act. He was sentenced in Denver, Colo., on October 28, 1940. Boarman was 24 years old, and his residence was in Indianapolis, Ind.

Floyd G. Hamilton, serving a 30 year sentence for violation of the National Bank Robbery Act, assault, and the National Motor Vehicle Theft Act. He was sentenced in November, 1938, at Fort Smith, Ark. He was a native of Dallas, Texas, and was 36 years old.

Fred Hunter, serving a sentence of 25 years, 10 months and nine days for assault and conspiracy to harbor Alvin Karpis, who at the time was wanted for kidnaping. He was sentenced at Cleveland. Hunter was 43 years old.

(OVER)

Mr. Bennett said that full details of the escape were not yet available. He said that Warden James A. Johnston of Alcatraz has reported, however, that the four men jumped into the bay from the rear of the model shop building. They were immediately spotted by prison officers on the roof of the building, who opened fire.

Brest was subsequently taken from the water by officers in the institutional launch shortly after releasing his hold on Boarman, who had been shot by the prison officers. Boarman's body sank at once. After his recapture, Brest told prison officials that he believed Hamilton, as well as Boarman, had been shot.

Since there were no boats in the vicinity of the men at the time of their jail break, Mr. Bennett said, it seems certain that the three missing prisoners were shot or drowned. The Coast Guard and the prison launch are continuing their patrol of the harbor in search of the bodies.

Later that day, Warden Johnston confidently told the press that Hamilton had evidently suffered the same fate as Boarman. But Hamilton had cheated death. After swimming as far as Little Alcatraz, he dove underwater, and dodging bullets, returned to the Rock, hiding behind a floating heap of rubber tires cast off from the mat shop in the same watery cave where the guards had found Hunter. Hamilton waited until nightfall and tried again to swim for it, but the bay's frigid water and turbulent currents defeated him. Weak from hunger and hypothermia, Hamilton gave up. Three days later, he climbed back up the cliff and sneaked in through the same bar-spread window he had jumped out of. Captain Weinhold, reexamining the scene of the escape, found the half-dead prisoner asleep next to a radiator. Covered in cuts and bruises, his underwear in tatters, Hamilton was a far cry from the swaggering public enemy who had terrorized the Southwest in the days of Bonnie and Clyde.

Reporters and photographers boarded a Coast Guard patrol boat for a first-hand view of the manhunt. The *San Francisco Chronicle* described the effort: "Starting from a distance, the Coast Guard, Alcatraz, and police boats would circle the area, coming closer on each loop until they came within a few yards of the Rock. At the Golden Gate, military police equipped with field glasses kept a careful watch on drifting objects in the water." Word of the escape traveled fast, and scores of curious people parked their cars along the waterfront to watch the search. On April 17, the media reported the news: "The Texas bad man scornful of life—others' lives, that is—crawled back into the prison building through the same hole he got out of."

In the years after the Alcatraz escape attempt, Hamilton became deeply religious and later served as vice president of the International Prison Ministry. Many years later, he founded an organization called ConAid, and received a full presidential pardon from Lyndon Johnson.

Little Alcatraz, a rocky outcrop marked by a buoy.

ESCAPE FILE 7

Escape 8

Now You See Me, Now You Don't

Escape artist tries disappearing act.

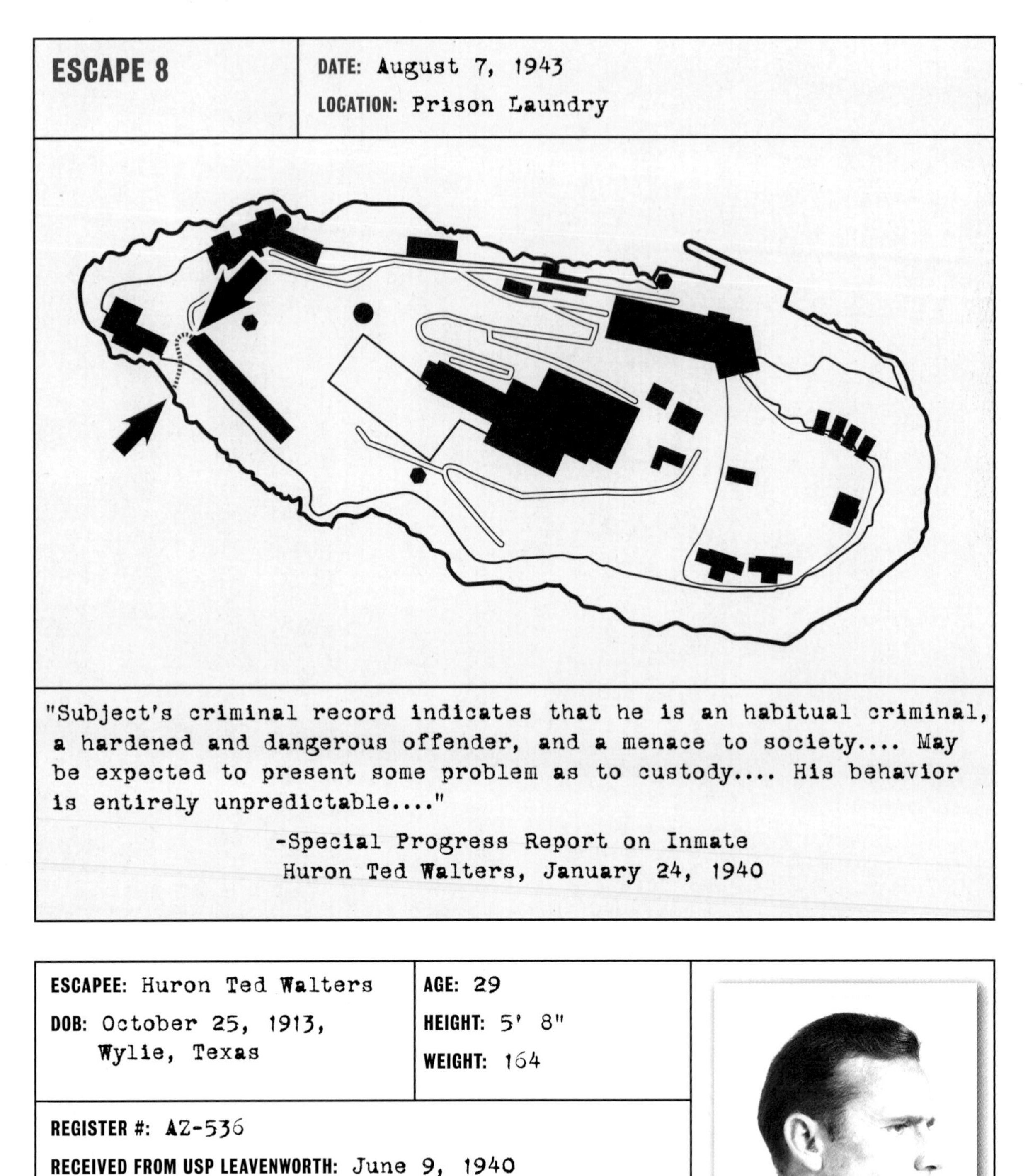

ESCAPE 8

DATE: August 7, 1943

LOCATION: Prison Laundry

"Subject's criminal record indicates that he is an habitual criminal, a hardened and dangerous offender, and a menace to society.... May be expected to present some problem as to custody.... His behavior is entirely unpredictable...."

-Special Progress Report on Inmate Huron Ted Walters, January 24, 1940

ESCAPEE: Huron Ted Walters

DOB: October 25, 1913, Wylie, Texas

AGE: 29

HEIGHT: 5' 8"

WEIGHT: 164

REGISTER #: AZ-536

RECEIVED FROM USP LEAVENWORTH: June 9, 1940

SENTENCE: 30 years for bank robbery, assault, and auto theft

REASON SENT TO ALCATRAZ: Repeated escape attempts

Most inmates joined forces to outsmart the island prison; generally, gangs of two, three, or four men constructed elaborate plots to get away. Only a rare few dared to go it alone, waging their own private battle of man vs. Alcatraz. Despite others' failures, Walters was determined to "get it right."

Road to Alcatraz

Ted Walters, AKA "Terrible Ted," of Native American and German descent, was the youngest of three children. Walters' parents had separated before he was born and his father, a farmer, died when he was two years old. His mother remarried a machinist two years later. Walters started school at age seven and left at age ten, having completed third grade. He regularly attended Sunday school and church.

At seventeen, Walters struck out on his own and worked as a truck driver. But soon, he began associating with criminals and stealing cars to supplement his income. Sent to the state penitentiary in Huntsville, Texas, in 1935, he escaped a year later, the first of many escapes—both attempted and successful—in his long criminal career.

On the loose, Walters hooked up with Floyd Hamilton and Jack Winn, and the three men began robbing banks, stores, beer taverns, and a Coca-Cola bottling plant. In June 1938, the trio robbed the Bank of Bradley in Bradley, Arkansas, and assaulted the cashier with loaded pistols. That August, they held up a salesman and stole his car. After a gun battle with state police, they escaped into the woods on foot. Winn, who was captured first, quickly gave up his accomplices. On November 5, 1938, Walters and Hamilton were each sentenced to thirty years and sent to Leavenworth. Before long, the two men plotted their escape from the institution, but another inmate alerted prison officials before they could put their plan into effect.

"This inmate [Walters] has a long dangerous record, and is one of the most vicious criminals in the Southwest and co-partner with Floyd Hamilton," wrote the associate warden at Leavenworth. Officials recommended that Walters and Hamilton be separated, and determined that Walters should be transferred to either Atlanta or Alcatraz. On June 9, 1940, Walters and Hamilton both arrived at Alcatraz, where each continued to buck the prison system, and each attempted to escape. In April 1943, Hamilton, along with three other inmates failed in his attempt to get off the island (see Escape File 7). Hamilton's unsuccessful escape proved no deterrent to Walters. He was determined to get it right.

ALCATRAZ AND WORLD WAR II

The island's Industries Building became a hub of activity for the war effort. The mat shop was converted into a cargo net factory. Inmates began manufacturing cold-weather field jackets and trousers for soldiers and maintained the buoys that kept the submarine nets in place. As inmate Ted Walters could attest, they did mountains of laundry for the military. They were paid a small wage for their work, and many invested in war bonds as a show of support. They cheered as battleships, cruisers, and destroyers headed out the Golden Gate for the South Pacific and took pride in their part in the war.

Once again, the US Army had a presence on the island. GIs manned antiaircraft guns on the prison's roof, waiting for the Japanese planes that never came. Air raid drills were instituted, during which a special siren was sounded and all lights on the island were turned off. For several years, young soldiers lived among prison officers and their families, enhancing the spirit of patriotism that had swept over the island.

Even contemporary culture took note: As Champ Larkin (played by James Craig) said in the 1942 movie, *Seven Miles from Alcatraz*, "We may be hoodlums, but we're American hoodlums."

The Plan

Walters was a keen observer of detail and a very patient man, two attributes he put to good use in plotting his escape. He had been working in the prison laundry for several years and, according to fellow inmate Jim Quillen, felt that its location outside the cellhouse walls offered some possibility of escape, if only he could find it. He eventually made several key discoveries. The first related to the war effort. There was a shortage of guards during

Prison laundry.

the war years, and officers in the laundry sometimes alternated rounds or left posts unattended for brief periods of time; also, the laundry was overwhelmed with the volume of military clothing delivered to the island. Second, he noticed that on Saturdays, guards manning the towers and walls focused their attention on the recreation yard rather than on the Prison Industries Building, since most of the inmates were in the yard.

Without arousing suspicion, Walters scored an assignment to work in the laundry on Saturday. There was plenty to be done and few inmates willing to give up weekend recreation breaks. Over time, he acquired a pair of wire cutters

Recreation yard.

and collected getaway clothing, which he stowed in one-gallon cans to be used as floats. All he had left to do was wait for the right moment to carry out his plan.

The Escape

On Saturday, August 7, 1943, while the guards had their eyes on the rec yard, Walters made his break. No one spotted the fast-moving convict as he slipped out of the laundry and made his way to what he hoped was freedom. The first problem arose when he attempted to cut through the heavy security fencing. No luck. Instead, he had to climb over two wire fences. As he started down the outside of the second fence, he lost his grip and fell, severely injuring his spine. But he refused to give up. In great pain, he made it down the steps to the water's edge and stripped to his underwear. He'd lost valuable time to the climb and the fall, and as he undressed, Walters heard the alarm siren shriek.

The Aftermath

Coast Guard boats joined the prison launch in a search. In less than an hour, Captain of the Guards Henry Weinhold and Associate Warden E. J. Miller found Walters, defeated, on the island's rocky shore. He had not even attempted to swim, realizing he couldn't navigate the icy waters in his condition. Walters did not resist the officers and was returned to the prison, where he spent ten days in the hospital before being placed in isolation and forfeiting 3,100 days of statutory good time. He hadn't made it off the island, but unlike some of the others who had attempted to escape, he lived to tell his tale.

In 1945, Walters returned to work in the laundry, but continued to rebel against prison life. Seven years later, he was transferred to USP Leavenworth, then to the Texas state prison system. Released in 1959, he spent the next ten-plus years bouncing in and out of prison. After taking a family hostage in October 1971, Walters was shot to death by a Texas Ranger.

The *San Francisco Chronicle* reported on the second escape attempt to take place in less than five months, reminding readers that "Alcatraz officials have long placed confidence in the cold, swirling waters about the prison as an effective barrier to freedom." No doubt Walters would have agreed.

JAMES V. BENNETT
DIRECTOR

DEPARTMENT OF JUSTICE

BUREAU OF PRISONS

WASHINGTON

August 9, 1943

MEMORANDUM

At 6:00 P.M. Saturday, August 7,1943, Alcatraz called me and Mr. Mills stated that a prisoner had been found missing in the laundry. He was seen ten minutes previous to the time his absence was discovered.

I told Mr. Mills that they would probably find the prisoner, and simply to let me have a telegram giving the information. The telegram was received at 7:00 P.M., reading:

> "Prisoner Walters reported as missing was located on beach about 3:45. Now in cell."

The Sunday Star carried the following clipping:

> "SAN FRANCISCO, Aug. 7. -- Ted H. Walters, a bank robber, attempted to escape from Alcatraz Federal Prison today but was caught by guards on the rocky edge of the island.
>
> "Warden J. A. Johnston said Walters, serving 30 years for bank robbery, automobile theft and assault in Fort Smith, Ark., sneaked out of the laundry building where he was working and climbed over a barbed-wire fence."

W. T. HAMMACK
Assistant Director

Escape 9

10-Year Escape Plan Succeeds

Identity thief takes boat off island.

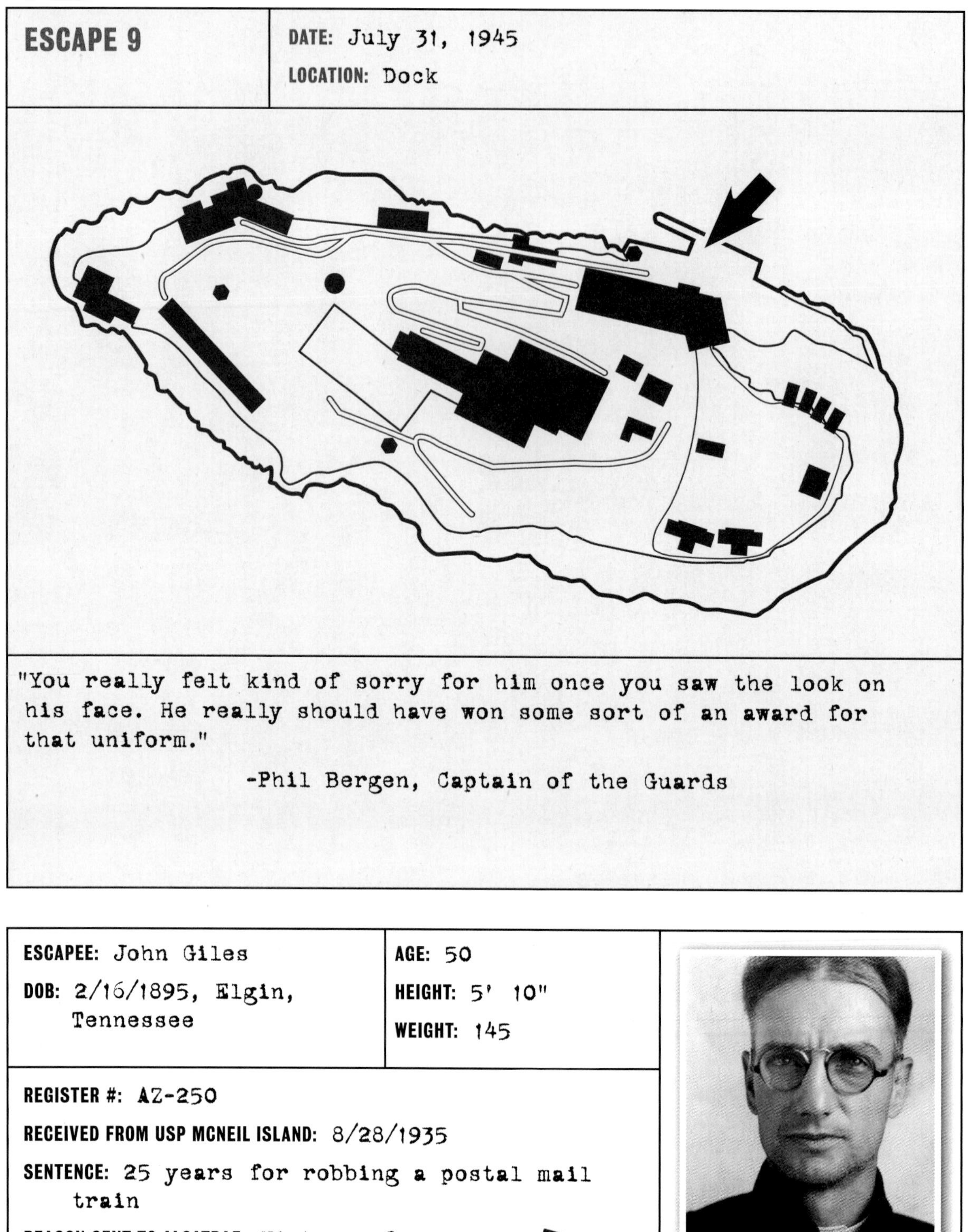

ESCAPE 9

DATE: July 31, 1945

LOCATION: Dock

"You really felt kind of sorry for him once you saw the look on his face. He really should have won some sort of an award for that uniform."

-Phil Bergen, Captain of the Guards

ESCAPEE: John Giles

DOB: 2/16/1895, Elgin, Tennessee

AGE: 50

HEIGHT: 5' 10"

WEIGHT: 145

REGISTER #: AZ-250

RECEIVED FROM USP MCNEIL ISLAND: 8/28/1935

SENTENCE: 25 years for robbing a postal mail train

REASON SENT TO ALCATRAZ: History of escape

Almost everything used at Alcatraz passed across the dock. Throughout the day, the area was a hive of activity, and convicts assigned to the docks were closely watched. But one inventive inmate managed to use his job as a dock worker to great advantage, and almost made it to freedom.

Road to Alcatraz

John Giles was the youngest of three boys. Records show that his mother was confined to a state hospital for mental illness for several years, and his parents apparently separated a number of times before finally divorcing when Giles was fifteen. He then left home and worked for four years as a surveyor's assistant with the US Bureau of Reclamation near British Columbia.

Giles' criminal life began when he was twenty. In 1915, he was convicted of robbery and incarcerated in the Washington State Penitentiary in Walla Walla. He was pardoned three years later, when the US entered World War I, most likely to allow him to enlist in the army. He apparently passed on the opportunity and in November 1918, robbed a bridge tender in Oregon. When a local deputy sheriff tried to arrest him, Giles shot and killed the lawman. Convicted of murder and given a life sentence, he returned to prison, this time, the state penitentiary in Salem, Oregon. Giles was a quiet inmate who served as a trusty (a convict considered trustworthy and allowed special privileges), earned some money writing short stories for pulp magazines, and was the editor of the prison magazine. Sixteen years into his sentence, he escaped. Asked years later what motivated him, he said, "I wrote fiction for magazines and the sources of my literary creation dimmed. I felt the need for new scenes and new faces. A sense of terrible futility came over me. So I went over the wall."

(Revised Feb., 1936)

RECORD OF COURT COMMITMENT

Original for Central File

Department of Justice

PENAL AND CORRECTIONAL INSTITUTIONS

UNITED STATES PENITENTIARY (copy)
(Institution)

ALCATRAZ, CALIFORNIA
(Location)

Inst. Name GILES, John K. No. 250-AZ

Alias Jack Sinclair, Basil Haig, J. K. Laird Color White Age 50 (2-16-95)

True Name John Knight Giles — Name and number of prior commitments to Fed. Inst. Same: #11539-McNeil Is., Wash.

Offense Post Office Violation-Assaulting Mail Custodian with Dangerous Weapon

District Utah - Salt Lake City

Sentence 25 Years (1-25 yrs & 1 3 yrs concurrent) Costs Fine none Committed Committed Not Committed Not Committed Paid Paid

Sentence changed New term Reason therefor

Sentenced . May 11, 1935 When arrested Feb. 15, 1935

Committed to Fed. Inst. . June 17, 1935 (McNeil Is.) Where arrested St. Paul, Minn.

Sentence begins . May 11, 1935 Residence Los Angeles, Calif.

Eligible for Parole . Sept. 10, 1943 Time in jail before trial From arrest

Eligible for conditional release with good time . ~~Feb. 22, 1952~~ see *Full term Rate per mo. good time 10 Total good time possible 3000 days

Eligible for con. rel. with extra good time . May 1, 1960 (Credit of 9 days industrial good time, to date)

Forfeited good time . August 2, 1945* Amount forfeited 3000 days(escape on boat)

Restoration good time . Amount restored

Expires full term . May 10, 1960 *

Former Com. on Sentence to Other Institutions

No.	Name of Institution	Location
7903	State Penitentiary	Salem, Oregon(Wanted)
7768	State Penitentiary	Walla Walla, Wash.

Person to be notified in case of serious illness or death

Name W. W. Giles
Relation to prisoner Brother
Address 2631 Locksley Pl., Los Angeles, Calif.
Telephone

Rec'd at Alcatraz Aug. 28, 1935 in transfer from USP, McNeil Is., Washington.

ACTION OF BOARD

Date	No. app.	Parole Forth.	Parole Effect.	Parole Rel.	Parole Den.	Parole Cont.	War. is.	Rev.	Dis. from par.
9-43	XXX								

Release and recommitments on present sentence other than parole

Date	Method
8-28-35	Trans. to Alcatraz
7-31-45	Escaped from Az, approx.10:20 a.m.Ret'd from Angel Is.,11:18a
10-1-45	WHC-Ad.P,N-Calif,Re
10-15-45	WHC-Ad.P,N-Calif,& Ret'd

DETAINERS FILED

Date	Nature of Detainer	Notify Whom	Remarks
10-9-35	For Escape from St.Pen.,	Salem, Oregon	

FPI—LK—4-15-41—22,500—3429-1

In May 1935, just seven months after his escape, Giles joined with six accomplices to rob the Denver and Rio Grande mail train in Salt Lake City. When he was captured, tried, and sentenced to spend another twenty-eight years at McNeil Island, prison authorities took his habit of escaping into account and recommended transfer to Alcatraz, where he arrived in August 1935. Warden Johnston described him as a deep and quiet gentleman with a lone-wolf personality.

Bright and with a keen eye for the details of prison operations, Giles missed few tricks. Once on the island, he quickly put in for a transfer, explaining that he'd heard Alcatraz was designated as the place for "irreclaimable incorrigibles" and that he was being classed as beyond redemption. He said he could behave himself in federal prison, but that he didn't belong with desperate and violent gangsters. A transfer, he claimed, would give him hope. It was not granted.

The Plan

Frail and physically weak, Giles was assigned to sweep the dock, unload military laundry, and tend the flowers that bordered the pathway. The job not only fit with his personality, it also gave him the chance to plot an escape the warden called one of the cleverest attempts he had ever seen. Over a period of nearly ten years, Giles used his access to incoming laundry to pilfer army clothing, shoulder patches, and even official dog tags.

The army vessel *General Frank M. Coxe* delivered laundry to Alcatraz from Fort McDowell on nearby Angel Island; once on Alcatraz, the soiled clothing was placed on a dock "shakedown" table and checked for contraband by one of the correctional officers. Prisoners then put the dirty clothing in bags for the Industries Building laundry operation. Patiently, stealthily, Giles stole one piece at a time and hid it in his jacket. When the army launch departed, Giles walked to the ramp area and swept up, which provided him with the perfect opportunity to pull out his loot and hide it in a canvas bag under the dock. By July 1945, after years of stealthy

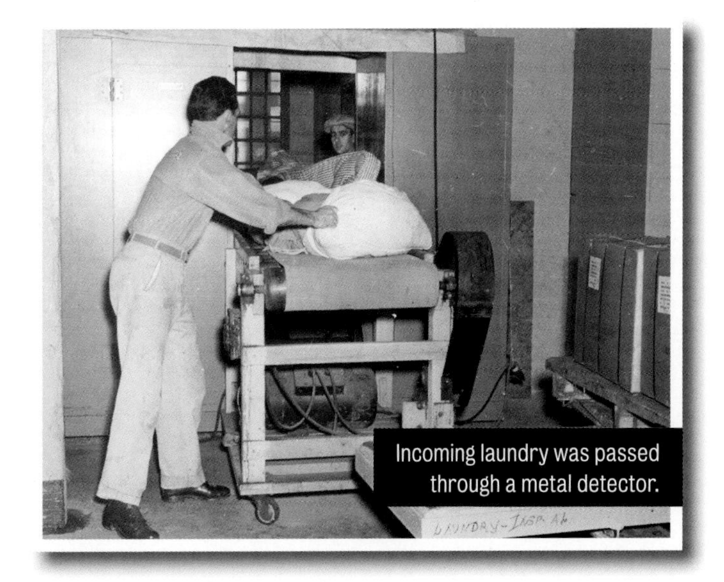

Incoming laundry was passed through a metal detector.

acquisition, he had acquired an entire Technical Sergeant's uniform and was ready to put his plan into action. Coincidentally, technicians from the US Army Signal Corps and the telephone company had been on and off the island for several weeks to repair a broken cable in the bay. They too arrived aboard the *General Coxe*, a fact Giles duly noted.

The Escape

On the morning of July 31, 1945, Giles reported to the dock as usual, then slipped away, retrieved his purloined uniform, changed into it, and pulled his prison coveralls on over it. He then went about his tasks until the *General Coxe* docked at 10:10 AM. As the boat came in, all the prisoners were lined up in their customary place and counted, as were the soldiers exiting onto the wharf. When the deckhands began offloading the cargo, Giles dropped unobserved below the dock, removed his coveralls, put on a cap, took a pencil and notebook from his pocket, and jumped aboard the boat through a freight hatchway. At the moment the whistle called prisoners back for another count, the lines were cast off and the steamer left the dock.

PIECE BY PIECE

As the cliché goes, "beggars can't be choosers," but John Giles' somewhat mismatched uniform worked well enough to get him off the island. Among the items he scored over the years:

- Regulation army tie
- Regulation army socks
- Regulation army shirt
- Regulation army pants
- Khaki army overseas cap
- Army field jacket, size 38L, with Technical Sergeant's chevron on sleeve
- Three sets of official US Army dog tags in the names of George F. Todd, Arthur Wade, and Ernest Bennett
- One enlisted man's temporary pass issued in the name of Todd
- Four enlisted man's temporary passes issued in the name of Wade
- Six blank enlisted man's passes
- Blank furlough paper, Form #31
- Assorted army shoulder patches and chevrons
- Grey flashlight and batteries
- Gold fountain pen
- Small medicine bottle containing ink
- Small memo book
- Texaco touring map of San Francisco and the Bay Area
- State Auto Association map of Marin County

Giles, who had been seen boarding the *Coxe*, was confronted by Corporal Paul Lorinz, who found him standing by himself in an out-of-the-way spot below deck and asked him, "Where are you going, Sergeant?" Lorinz recalled that Giles, who wouldn't look directly at him, said he was headed to Fort McDowell. Lorinz continued to question Giles, who claimed that he was a lineman working on the cable. He then pulled out a notebook and acted as though he were making notes.

BOAT FELON HID ON

Corporal Paul Lorinz (left) and Sergeant Shirley Casey point to lower deck of Army ferryboat General Coxe on which John K. Giles hid after escape from Alcatraz today. On upper deck is Deck Hand Jerry Van Soest; below, Oiler Jim Saunders. Lorinz spotted Giles as prisoner despite the fact he was wearing Army uniform and Giles was seized when ferry put in at Angel Island. —Call-Bulletin Photograph.

Giles' bold attempt made the news across the country.

Back at Alcatraz, Giles' absence was discovered almost immediately. After searching the dock area from top to bottom—including under the dock itself—the officers phoned Associate Warden E. J. Miller. The escape siren was still shrieking on Alcatraz as Miller raced to Angel Island on one of the prison boats and the warden radioed the Coast Guard and the San Francisco Police Department to get boats on the bay. Johnston also phoned army headquarters on Angel Island and told officers there to hold all *Coxe* passengers for inspection.

Associate Warden Miller arrived just after the *Coxe* had tied up. Following the warden's request, Lieutenant Kilgore, Officer of the Day at Fort McDowell, had lined up a group of soldiers whose passes he questioned. Miller walked down the line, took a good look at Giles, and snapped the handcuffs on him. Giles' brief moment of freedom ended at 11 AM. Before noon, he was back at Alcatraz.

The Aftermath

Giles—who was found to have stolen more than forty items to aid his escape (see sidebar)—was checked into the prison, given his inmate clothes, and placed in solitary confinement. That afternoon, he was interviewed by FBI agents, and

UNITED STATES PENITENTIARY
ALCATRAZ, CALIFORNIA

CONDUCT REPORT

NAME GILES, JOHN K.   NO. 250-AZ.

DATE REPORTED	OFFENSE AND ACTION
11-2-36	FIGHTING WITH #257-Hensley. This inmate fought with inmate #257-Hensley. They were striking vicious blows at each other and refused to stop when requested. I seperated them twice and each time they started swinging at each other again. W.B.Cotteral, Jr. C.O. ACTION: To be placed in Solitary Confinement on restricted diet "A" Block and to forfeit all privileges until further orders. C.J.Shuttleworth, Deputy Warden.
11-5-36	**Giles #250-AZ. is to be released from Solitary Confinement to regular cell with the loss off all privileges until further orders, effective 3 P.M. this date. C.J.Shuttleworth, Deputy Warden.**
11-13-36	**All privileges are hereby restored to Giles-#250-AZ. effective this date. C. J. Shuttleworth, Deputy Warden.**
10-26-41	ATTACKING ANOTHER INMATE. As the line was coming from the dining room Gil went beyond his cell to hit Moreland, #77-AZ. Moreland did not hit back he held Giles until I got there. Report by Ozarkiewitz, Sr. Officer. ACTION: Inmate Giles admitted the he was wrong and that he swung at Morel as he thought that Moreland had stolen something from his cell. Moreland on being questioned also said that Giles had made a mistake. They both apoogized and were very friendly. Moreland was sent back to his cell. Giles was put insolitary confinement in "A" Block. E. J. Lloyd, Associate Warden.
10-28-41	Removed to regular cell and work assignment.
7-31-45	**ATTEMPTED ESCAPE. Having in his possession contraband clothing and other articles, purloined from laundry-shake down on dock, including coat, shirt, trousers, cap, necktie, squadron patches, insigna, identification tags, passes and forms for passes, as worn and used by soldiers in the U.S. Army; dressing himself in the contraband clothing so as to appear and represent himself as a Technical sergeant, U.S. Army; writing a fictitious temporary pass to correspond with the Army identification tag that he was wearing; leaving his place of assignment on the dock, going under the dock and jumping from stringers under dock to the cargo hatch of the steamer Frank H. Coxe and riding on the Coxe to Angel Island in attempt to escape; all of the above occurred about and between 10:00 a.m. and 11:00 a.m., Tuesday, July 31, 1945. Report #38880, E.J. Miller, Associate Warden.** **ACTION: Made no statement, but acknowledged the known facts. Was apprehended on Angel Island and returned to Alcatraz. Isolation on restricted diet, loss of all privileges and to be tried by the Good Time Board.** **7-31-45 E. J. Miller, Associate Warden.** 8-2-45: FORFEITURE OF 3000 DAYS STATUTORY GOOD TIME, AFTER TRIAL BY GOOD TIME TRIAL BOARD, 8-2-45. 8-7-45: Removed from solitary to Isolation D-cell; 8-15-45 to Hospital 8-19-45 Ret'd to D-Seg.

was less than forthcoming with the agents: "It's not in my book to tell the officers anything, because I don't want to injure the chances that another prisoner may have of escaping if he can plan it and make it." As far as Giles was concerned, it was up to the prison officers to keep him in, and up to him to get away if he could.

When Giles got out of D Block three years later, he was given incinerator detail, considered one of the island's worst jobs. He also forfeited 3,000 days of good-time credit and was sentenced to another three years in Alcatraz; since his first incarceration (in 1915), he had been free little more than a year altogether.

Giles in his purloined uniform.

John Giles was one of only two inmates who made it off the island and lived to tell the story, and his attempt made front-page news. The story of Giles' attempted escape and capture were also profiled on the radio program *Gang Busters* in 1945. Two decades later, MGM, the studio that financed and distributed the 1967 film, *Point Blank*, made two quirky documentary shorts to promote the film, one of which features John Giles, 77 years old at the time. In the short (which can be seen on the re-released DVD) Giles spoke of his time on the Rock: "Everything was so strict. A man with a long time, he's got only one thought—he wants to escape, needs to escape. You think it's the end of your life. You don't want to die in prison. You have that obsession. That's all you think about. It fills your waking hours from morning to night."

Escape 10

Battle of Alcatraz

Bloody uprising rages
in cellhouse—2 guards,
3 prisoners slain.

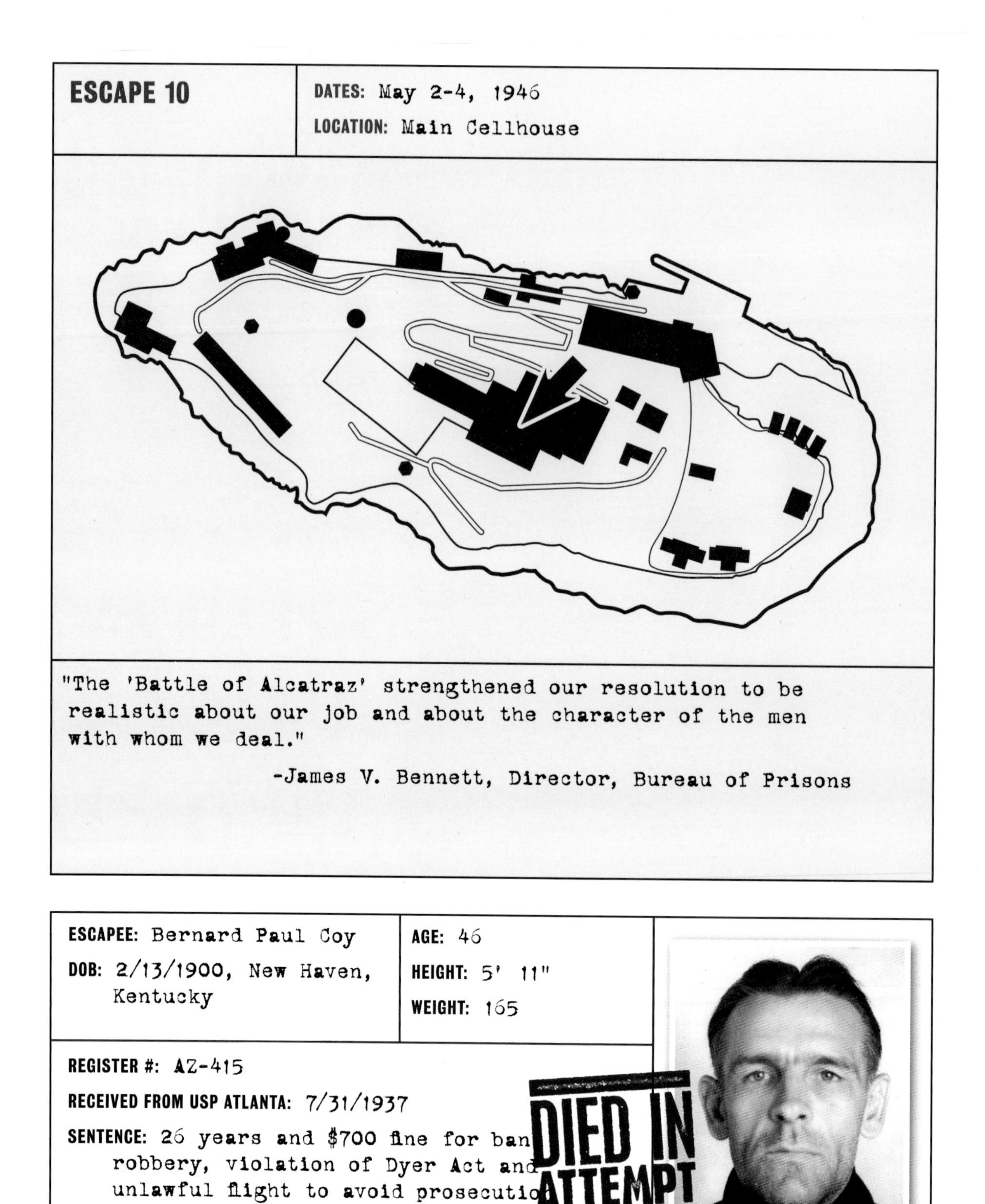

ESCAPE 10

DATES: May 2-4, 1946

LOCATION: Main Cellhouse

"The 'Battle of Alcatraz' strengthened our resolution to be realistic about our job and about the character of the men with whom we deal."

-James V. Bennett, Director, Bureau of Prisons

ESCAPEE: Bernard Paul Coy

DOB: 2/13/1900, New Haven, Kentucky

AGE: 46

HEIGHT: 5' 11"

WEIGHT: 165

REGISTER #: AZ-415

RECEIVED FROM USP ATLANTA: 7/31/1937

SENTENCE: 26 years and $700 fine for ban robbery, violation of Dyer Act and unlawful flight to avoid prosecutio

REASON SENT TO ALCATRAZ: Length of sentence, criminal record, violent nature of crimes

The most violent escape attempt in the history of Alcatraz was engineered by six of the prison's most dangerous and intractable inmates. After the bloody siege came to an end, three of the prisoners who fought desperately to escape finally left the island—in body bags.

Road to Alcatraz

Bernie Coy, who was neglected as a child, had a violent temper and was harshly punished. At five, he began stealing money from his mother's purse. By nine, he was in custody for stealing auto parts. In 1916, his life took a new direction when he enlisted in the army and during World War I, served with distinction. After the war, he went AWOL, was charged with assault and battery, and eventually served five years in state prison for bank robbery. In 1937, armed with a sawed-off

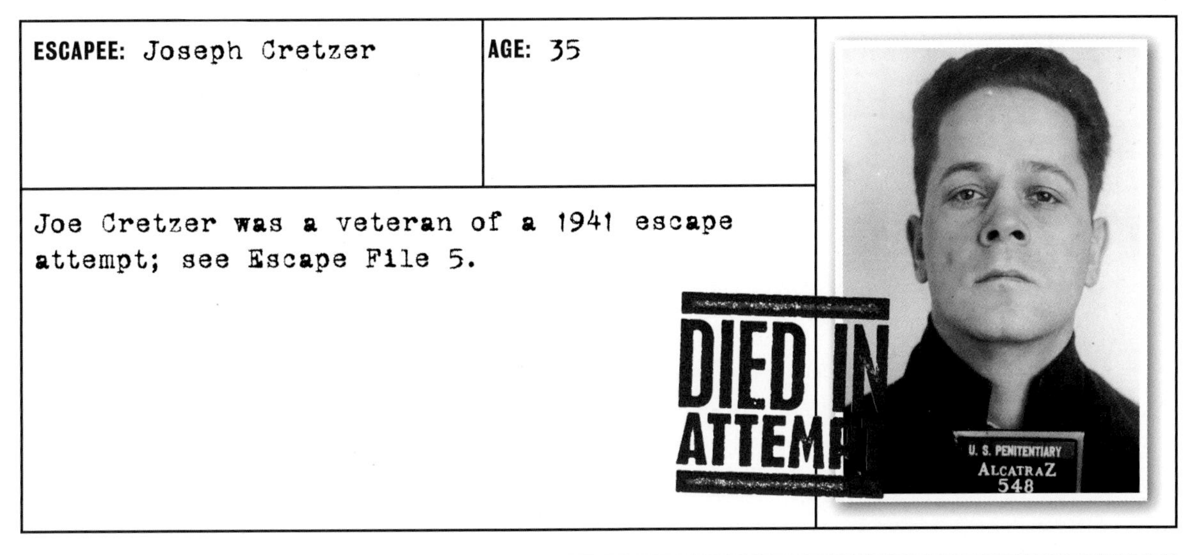

ESCAPEE: Joseph Cretzer

AGE: 35

Joe Cretzer was a veteran of a 1941 escape attempt; see Escape File 5.

ESCAPEE: Marvin Franklin Hubbard **DOB:** 8/13/1912, Boaz, Alabama	**AGE:** 33 **HEIGHT:** 5' 8" **WEIGHT:** 143	U. S. PENITENTIARY ALCATRAZ 645 12 7 44
REGISTER #: AZ-645 **RECEIVED FROM USP ATLANTA:** 1944 **SENTENCE:** 30 years for kidnapping a Tennessee policeman, auto theft, gun theft **REASON SENT TO ALCATRAZ:** Involvement in prison riot, escape risk		DIED IN ATTEMPT

shotgun, he stole $2,175 from the National Bank of Kentucky. Incarcerated in Atlanta, he brutally attacked another inmate. His punishment was a one-way ticket to the Rock. Coy never accepted prison life; he spent most of his time reading psychology, painting landscapes, and dreaming of escape. When a writ of habeas corpus seeking his release from Alcatraz was denied, he confided to an inmate, "Now, I got nothing to lose." He spent his time searching for flaws in the prison's security system, convinced he could bust his way out.

For **Joe Cretzer**'s background, see Escape File 5. Here's how other cons saw him, according to Jim Quillen (AZ-586): "Joe was, in all respects, what a convict was reputed to be. He was young, but also recognized by all as a man of his word in the world of prisons. He was tough and violent, a leader for those who wished to be led and above all, unafraid to face the consequences of his actions. He was felt to be too impulsive and impatient by many of the older, escape-minded inmates, and as a consequence, died for his actions."

"Meek Marvin" Hubbard was a stocky, barrel-chested country boy who dropped out of school to work on the family farm. At ten, he ran away to live with a relative, who trained him in the art of bricklaying. Then, when he was seventeen, after a string of robberies and a brief stint behind bars, he teamed up with other criminals and began committing violent crimes. He and his accomplices stole at gunpoint, kidnapped several individuals (including a police officer), and landed in the Knox County Jail in Knoxville, Tennessee. He overpowered a jailhouse guard, but was captured by the sheriff three days later. Sent to the federal penitentiary in Atlanta, he joined in a prison riot. His next—and final—stop was Alcatraz.

The youngest of six children, **Miran "Buddy" Thompson** was a delinquent

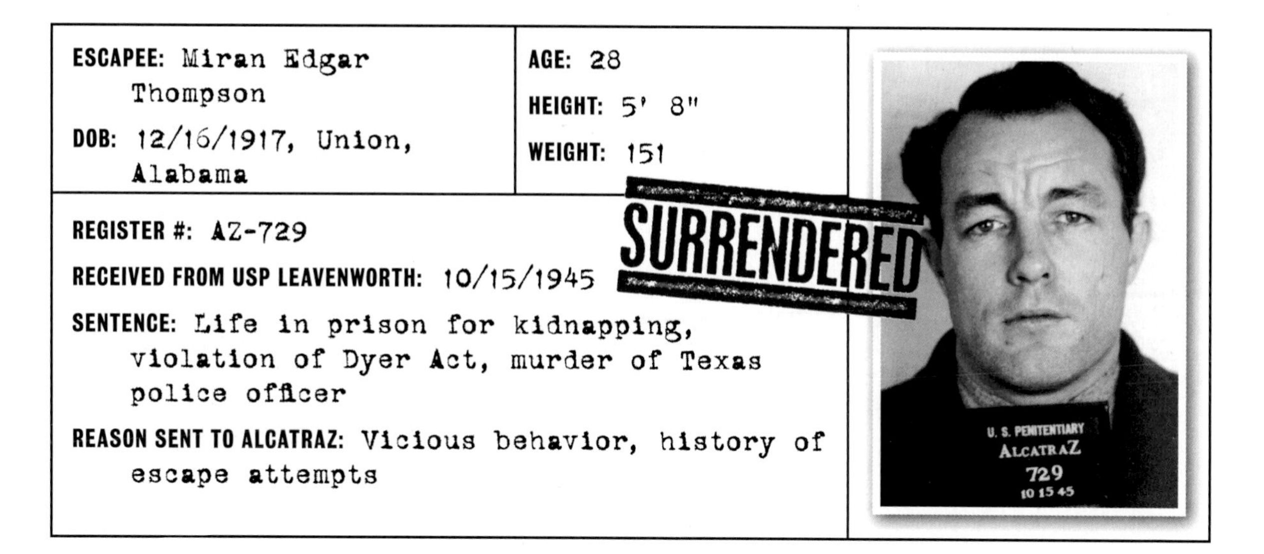
ESCAPEE: Miran Edgar Thompson

DOB: 12/16/1917, Union, Alabama

AGE: 28

HEIGHT: 5' 8"

WEIGHT: 151

REGISTER #: AZ-729

RECEIVED FROM USP LEAVENWORTH: 10/15/1945

SENTENCE: Life in prison for kidnapping, violation of Dyer Act, murder of Texas police officer

REASON SENT TO ALCATRAZ: Vicious behavior, history of escape attempts

SURRENDERED

by the age of ten. He served time in an Alabama reformatory for armed robbery, and escaped five times. Over the next few years, he accumulated a long list of offenses throughout the South, including larceny, assault, forgery, burglary, and motor-vehicle theft. Arrested in Texas for burglarizing a store, Thompson shot and killed the Amarillo police officer who had neglected to spot a handgun hidden in his pants. The deputy marshal who delivered him to Leavenworth considered Thompson such a dangerous criminal that he drove straight through from Amarillo to the Kansas prison rather than risk an overnight stop. Thompson had a record of eight escape attempts by the time he was transferred to Alcatraz in 1945. His record as a vicious cop-killer gave him special status among the island's other inmates.

For **Sam Shockley**'s background, see Escape File 5.

ESCAPEE: Sam Richard Shockley

AGE: 37

Shockley may have been a veteran of a 1941 escape attempt; see Escape File 5.

SURRENDERED

ESCAPEE: Clarence Victor Carnes DOB: 1/14/1927, Daisy, Oklahoma	AGE: 19 HEIGHT: 5' 10" WEIGHT: 150
REGISTER #: AZ-714 RECEIVED FROM USP LEAVENWORTH: 7/8/1945 SENTENCE: Life plus 99 years for kidnapping, robbery, and murder REASON SENT TO ALCATRAZ: Serious discipline problems and history of escape attempts	

SURRENDERED

Clarence Carnes, a full-blooded Choctaw Indian, was raised in a poverty-stricken, Depression-era family in Oklahoma and committed his first crime at the age of eight: breaking into the school canteen and stealing candy and money. By the time he was in his teens, he was a gang leader. Carnes got into serious trouble at fifteen, when he held up a gas station and killed the attendant. He received a life sentence for murder, but in 1945, escaped from a Granite Reformatory chain gang. He and two accomplices stole a car, kidnapped the owner, and drove across state lines. Once recaptured, he was sentenced to ninety-nine years in prison and sent to Leavenworth. Another escape attempt earned him a transfer to Alcatraz, where he became the youngest inmate ever sent to the island penitentiary. The eighteen-year-old was described as impulsive and aggressive, not one to back down in the face of trouble. As the prison psychiatric summary concluded, "It is possible he may develop emotional maturity as time goes by, but this cannot be counted on with any certainty."

The Plan

Coy firmly believed that to break the Rock, he and his fellow escapees had to arm themselves with guns. His meticulous plan, years in the making, relied on this basic premise. It would be the first—and only—time an Alcatraz prisoner got his hands on a firearm.

In 1945, Coy managed to secure an assignment as a cellhouse orderly, which gave him access to most of the main cellblock. This relative freedom allowed him to spot a tiny flaw in one of the prison's security features. With the proper tools, the bars of the gun gallery overlooking the cellhouse could be spread wide enough to slip through, enabling him to steal weapons from an unsuspecting guard. Coy's job also gave him plenty of time to study the rotations and habits of various officers. With this information in hand, Coy designed a bold offensive: overpower the cellhouse guards and steal their guns and keys, free his co-conspirators, find the key to the recreation yard, and get outside the cellhouse walls. At that point, they would shoot the tower guards, flee to the dock, and commandeer the prison launch, which he and his fellow escapees would use to cross the bay to the mainland and disappear forever. He was prepared to take guards and/or their family members hostage if necessary.

Coy carefully recruited a small army of accomplices: Joe Cretzer and Sam Shockley, both veterans of a failed escape, as well as Marvin Hubbard, Clarence Carnes, and Miran Thompson. With help from numerous other inmates, he acquired and stashed a number of tools in the cellhouse, and fashioned a makeshift bar spreader from brass toilet parts (see sidebar). To prepare for the assault on the gun gallery, Coy lost twenty pounds to make it easier to get through the bars. Finally, he arranged for "Crazy Sam" Shockley to create a disturbance in D Block. That would set the whole escape plan in motion.

The Escape

It was May 2, 1946. The time was 1:40 PM. Coy was polishing the cellhouse floor. Officer Bert Burch was stationed in the West Gun Gallery. Officer William Miller was patrolling

THE BAR SPREADER

The Battle of Alcatraz could not have happened if Coy had not been able to spread the bars to gain access to the gun gallery. The ingenious bar spreader had been surreptitiously made in a prison workshop, then smuggled into the cellhouse in the false bottom of a garbage can. Consisting of rods and screws from a toilet mechanism, it was assembled to fit within the five-inch space between two parallel bars. Each end of the rod was notched so it could be firmly seated. Rotating the nut with pliers applied pressure to the bars, bending and forcing them apart. It is believed that the cellhouse plumber (Ed Mrozik, AZ-607) smuggled the pliers to Coy and helped make the tool that was so essential to the escape plot.

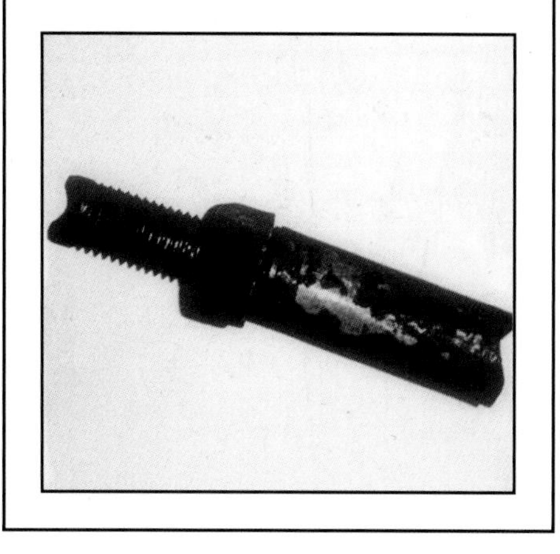

C Block and Officer Cecil Corwin was keeping watch in D Block. On a cue from Coy, Shockley started yelling, cursing, and raising a ruckus. Officer Burch walked down to the end of the gallery and crossed over into D Block, which was separated from the main cellhouse by a concrete wall. At that moment, Coy signaled to Hubbard, who had been working kitchen detail. Hubbard came to the door of the cellhouse and indicated that he wished to return to his cell, and Officer Miller opened the door. Coy and Hubbard (armed with a knife he had stolen from the kitchen) jumped Officer Miller, dragged him into nearby cell 403, and took his keys. The cons immediately racked open the doors of the cells housing Cretzer, Thompson, and Carnes, who had remained inside that afternoon instead of reporting for work duty. So far, the escape was on schedule.

Coy sprinted down C Block to retrieve the tool bag he had hidden in the utility corridor. He removed his clothes and, with Cretzer's help, smeared axle grease on his skinny torso; climbed the outside bars of the gun gallery; and, using the bar spreader, opened the bars and painfully squeezed through. When Officer Burch returned from D Block, Coy ambushed him and knocked him out, then lowered the guard's keys and a .45 automatic to his colleagues. Entering the D Block gallery, he ordered Officer Corwin to open the door between segregation and the main cellhouse; once he complied, the guard was marched to cell 403 and locked in with Officer Miller. Though Cretzer was able to free Shockley and other inmates on the top two tiers of D Block, he was unable to open the interior doors to the isolation cells on the bottom row. After releasing the steel exterior doors, he left the area in frustration.

Correctional officer points to the spot Coy slipped through the bars into the gun gallery.

The cellhouse under siege.

Meanwhile, in the gun gallery, Coy stripped Officer Burch of his uniform and bound him, then passed clubs, tear-gas grenades, gas masks, ammunition, and the rifle to Hubbard and lowered himself to the cellhouse floor. One after another, guards who came to the cellhouse were overpowered and confined to cells.

But there had been one fatal slip. Although the prisoners had secured two weapons, they were missing the most important item: Key 107, which opened the door leading to the recreation yard. Earlier, in violation of standard procedures, Officer Miller had slipped that key into his pocket; once in cell 403, he hid it in the toilet. The clock was ticking and Coy and his men were desperate to open the door to the rec yard. One after another, they tried all the keys on the guard's ring—no luck. When they finally searched the cell and located the key, it was too late; in their panic, they forced it into the lock, which jammed the mechanism (as it was designed to do). They were trapped.

Cretzer went berserk. Armed with Officer Burch's .45, he fired at the guards through the cell bars. Officer Miller was killed and several others were wounded. Finally alerted to the trouble, Warden Johnston sounded the alarm and radioed the San Francisco police and Coast Guard for help. While

The narrow utility corridor in which the bodies of Coy, Cretzer, and Hubbard were found.

ESCAPE FILE 10

guards herded 150 prisoners out of the prison shops and into the yard, other prisoners crouched in their cells. The guards then stormed into the cellhouse long enough to rescue their fellow officers. In the melee, Officer Harold Stites was shot and killed by "friendly" fire.

Out in the bay, police boats circled the island. A company of marines landed and began firing rifle grenades into the cellblock. Climbing to the roof, they proceeded to drill holes and drop grenades through to the floor below. From inside came explosions and rifle fire, and the cellhouse filled with smoke and tear gas. The waterlines broke, spewing water into the cells. Army planes swooped and dived over the Rock, and thousands lined the city's shoreline for a glimpse of the prison mutiny. The battle raged for almost forty-five hours before it was finally contained. At 9:40 AM on Saturday, May 4, guards stormed the prison and found the bodies of Coy, Cretzer, and Hubbard in a utility corridor. Stiff in rigor mortis, Coy lay with his arms cocked as though holding a rifle; Cretzer and Hubbard were close by. Carnes, Shockley, and Thompson had lost their nerve and crawled back into their cells.

L to R: Carnes, Shockley, and Thompson on their way to court.

The Aftermath

After the rebellion ended, guards struggled through the heavily damaged cellblock and rounded up Shockley, Thompson, and Carnes. Two guards—Miller and Stites—were dead, and thirteen had been wounded. For the first time in a dozen years, Warden Johnston allowed the press into the penitentiary. He toured reporters and photographers

Contemporary news illustration.

through what had been a bloody war zone, describing the brutal escape attempt in great detail and ignoring the inmates who shouted at him from their cells.

In November 1946, Thompson, Shockley, and Carnes were hauled into federal court for the murder of Officer Miller. After a sensational trial, the three men were found guilty of first-degree murder. Thompson and Shockley were sentenced to death and executed in San Quentin's gas chamber with an Alcatraz prison guard among the witnesses. When it was over, the guard commented: "That makes it five to two. It's a little more even now." Nineteen-year-old Carnes' life was spared, as he had refused to kill the guards held hostage, but he had a second life sentence added to his original life sentence, plus ninety-nine years. In the end, Carnes spent almost his entire adult life behind bars; he died in 1988 and was interred in a pauper's grave on Indian land in Oklahoma.

Stories of the "Battle of Alcatraz" appeared on the front pages of more than 600 US newspapers and countless more around the world. On May 4, 1946, the *Oregon Journal* summed it up: "Convicts in great prisons who stage riots in escape attempts seldom accomplish anything by their ill-advised and usually tragic outbreaks. Yet such outbreaks are understandable. The men are simply

Bodies of Hubbard, Coy, and Cretzer in the San Francisco city morgue.

stir-crazy. They . . . are humiliated by their loss of liberty, resentful over real or fancied disciplinary injustices; they brood over the idea that they have been falsely incarcerated. . . . Crime-hardened men, maddened by confinement, became savages in the Alcatraz break."

The saga of the Battle of Alcatraz lives on in film. Among the cinematic versions are the television dramas *Alcatraz, the Whole Shocking Story* (1980) and *Six Against the Rock* (1987).

IN REPLYING. ADDRESS THE
CHIEF MEDICAL OFFICER

FEDERAL SECURITY AGENCY

U. S. PUBLIC HEALTH SERVICE

UNITED STATES PENITENTIARY

ALCATRAZ, CALIFORNIA

May 6, 1946.

Medical Director,
Bureau of Prisons,
Department of Justice,
Washington, D. C.

Sir:

I regret to have to inform you of the death of three inmates whose names you will find listed below.

Joseph Paul Cretzer AZ-548.
Pronounced dead at 10:22 A.M. on May 4, 1946.
Died of penetrating wound of left temporal region, and large gaping wound anterior right ear.

Bernard Paul Coy, AZ-415
Pronounced dead at 10:12 A.M. May 4, 1946.
Cause of death Penetrating wound of left maxilla and penetrating wound left border sternal mastoid muscle.

Marvin Franklin Hubbard, AZ-645
Pronounced dead at 10:16 A.M. May 4, 1946.
Cause of death Penetrating wound left temporal region. Penetrating wound above left eyelid and below the brow. Large gaping wound right posterior temporal occipital region.

The above inmates died as result of riot on May 2,1946 through May 4, 1946 and the exact time of death cannot be determined.

Respectfully,

Louis G. Roucek, Surgeon(R)
Chief Medical Officer.

LGR/jar

Escape 11

Rubber Tire Bonfire Screens Getaway

Hard-luck gunman reaches the end of his rope.

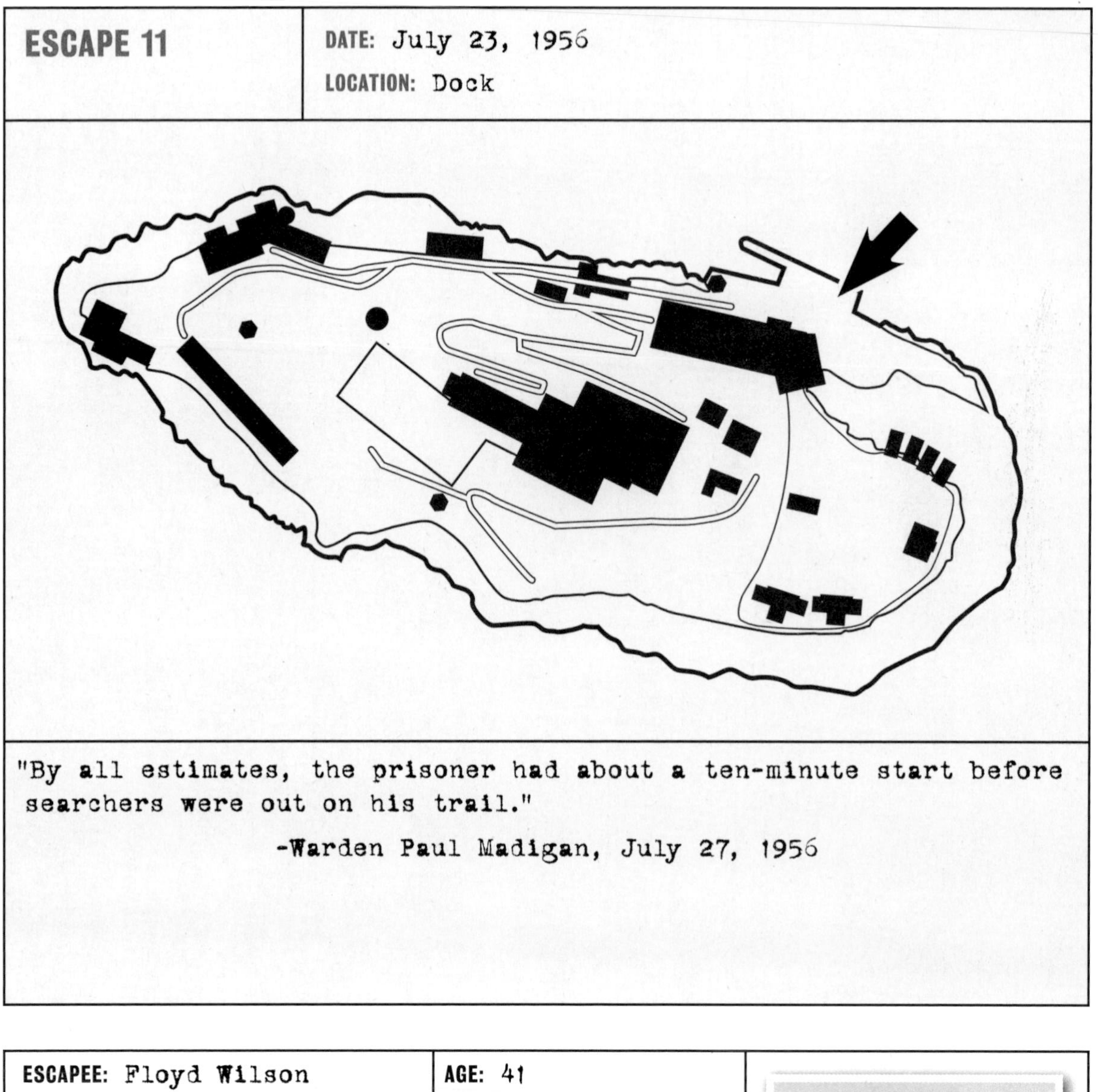

ESCAPE 11

DATE: July 23, 1956

LOCATION: Dock

"By all estimates, the prisoner had about a ten-minute start before searchers were out on his trail."

-Warden Paul Madigan, July 27, 1956

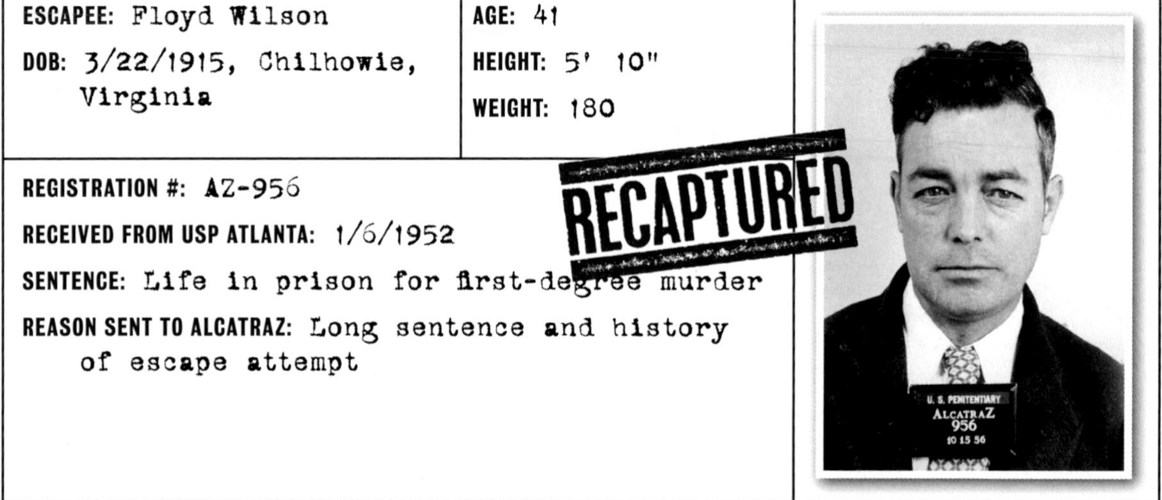

ESCAPEE: Floyd Wilson

DOB: 3/22/1915, Chilhowie, Virginia

AGE: 41

HEIGHT: 5' 10"

WEIGHT: 180

REGISTRATION #: AZ-956

RECEIVED FROM USP ATLANTA: 1/6/1952

SENTENCE: Life in prison for first-degree murder

REASON SENT TO ALCATRAZ: Long sentence and history of escape attempt

Warden Johnston retired in 1948, and his successors loosened the rigid routine. Despite attempts to make life on Alcatraz a little more tolerable, almost every prisoner longed for freedom. A former inmate summed it up: "Nothing could blot out the . . . certainty that this was all life held for you in the future."

Road to Alcatraz

Floyd Wilson was raised with four sisters and a brother. He completed sixth grade before quitting school to help his father, who was an interior decorator. In 1947, when he was a jobless carpenter with a wife and five children age eighteen months to nine years, Wilson set out from his home in a Washington, D.C., suburb to get $17 to buy a ton of coal "so my kids won't freeze to death." He shot and killed a young store employee who was driving to a local bank to make a cash deposit of $10,162. Wilson panicked and fled the scene, leaving the money behind. When he was picked up at his home shortly thereafter, he said he had not intended to kill.

Wilson was sentenced to death for first-degree murder, but, sympathetic to Wilson's case, President Harry Truman commuted the sentence to life in prison. He entered the federal penitentiary in Atlanta in 1949 and almost immediately set out to escape. He managed to get his hands on a rope and some pipe segments, but was discovered with the contraband. Unlucky again, he was transferred to Alcatraz.

Like many inmates, Wilson never adjusted to life in the pen. He was considered uncommunicative and surly, failed to follow officers' instructions, and did not get along with fellow workers. Showing no interest in sports, he seldom went to the recreation yard and when he did, he talked only to guards and to a few

RULE #51: VISITS

"You are allowed to receive one visit each month from members of your immediate family or other persons approved by the Warden."

During Wilson's time on Alcatraz, it appears that he received infrequent visits from a niece who lived in Sacramento, California, and that his mother visited only once.

Like every other aspect of life on Alcatraz, visits were tightly regulated. None were allowed during the inmate's first three months of incarceration; after that, and only with good behavior and prior approval of the warden, convicts were allowed one visitor per month. Visits were limited to two hours.

Upon arriving on the island, visitors had to pass through a metal detector at the dock. Each person emptied his or her pockets, took off eyeglasses, and removed anything else that contained metal. For one prominent visitor, this strict procedure proved highly embarrassing. As Al Capone's mother stepped through the metal detector, the buzzer immediately sounded. The guard then took her purse, but the reaction was the same. Finally, the guard called for the associate warden's wife, who searched the visitor in a private room. She discovered that Mrs. Capone's corset had metal stays. Once Mrs. Capone removed the stays, she was able to pass through the gate—but she never visited again.

At the cellhouse, visitors were not allowed any physical contact with the inmate. They could only see each other through a thick sheet of bulletproof glass, and communicate via telephone intercom. Guards monitored every word of the conversation and were quick to cut off any discussion of current events, prison conditions, or crime. Inmates dubbed the visiting area "Pekin' [Peeking] Place."

of the older inmates. Wilson repeatedly begged for a transfer to an East Coast prison so he could be closer to his children. (According to his annual review in 1962, Wilson said it had been many years since he had seen members of his family, and he felt quite forsaken.)

The Plan

Wilson worked on the dock for several years, where he was assigned to the garbage detail. He somehow acquired a twenty-five-foot length of cord, which he planned to use to put together a raft from driftwood on the beach. With rope in hand and a rough plan in mind, Wilson waited for his chance to slip away.

The Escape

That chance came on the afternoon of July 23, 1956. At 3:25 PM—when both the prison launch and the water barge were about to leave—the inmates were called on the line for a head count. Wilson was present. At 3:50 PM, the launch returned, another line-up was staged, and Wilson was gone. Officer Jones later reported that he saw Wilson throw a rubber auto tire on a bonfire he had been tending at the end of the dock. Black smoke billowed into the sky, perhaps creating a screen for Wilson to slip away from the dock gang and head to the water's edge.

Dock guard tower.

The Aftermath

Wilson's attempted escape set off a massive manhunt. All police departments and sheriff's offices in the nine San Francisco Bay Area counties were alerted to watch for the convict, and police radios monotonously intoned Wilson's description: 5' 10" tall, 180 pounds, deep suntan, bright blue eyes, wearing a prison blue work shirt and blue jeans. Special detachments of Military Police beat the brush at Fort Mason. Two Coast Guard patrol craft circled the Rock, their searchlights probing the water, watching for a bobbing head. And on Alcatraz, teams of FBI agents and correctional officers began an inch-by-inch search. More

than sixty-five men scoured the entire island from 4 PM until after midnight. As it got dark, floodlights were set up to illuminate the east end of the island.

At first, the searchers thought Wilson had slipped onto the water barge and ridden it across the bay. But soon after the search began, they found an area near the bonfire where the fence had been pried up. By all estimates, Wilson had only about a ten-minute start before searchers were on his trail.

At 2:55 AM, the convict was found, cold and wet, in a crevice about thirty feet from the beach, on the east side of the island. He had managed to avoid detection for more than twelve hours. In a formal report to the director of the Bureau of Prisons, Warden Madigan stated, "We have one satisfaction of knowing that our procedure was tight enough to prevent any of these men from getting on the water barge, but we are red-faced in the fact that Wilson eluded us for the number of hours that he did."

Wilson was returned to isolation and all privileges forfeited. He was prosecuted for attempted escape, but a lenient jury found him not guilty. He remained at Alcatraz until it closed in 1963, when he was transferred to the federal penitentiary in Atlanta, then to Lorton Reformatory in Virginia. Finally paroled in 1971, he returned to Maryland and resumed his work as a carpenter. Parole officers reported that "Floyd Wilson led a rather quiet and orderly life since his release. . . . He visits with relatives, enjoys sports, and engages in other reputable pursuits when not working."

Local newspapers closely covered Wilson's disappearance. Early on, they suggested that the convicted murderer had been the first to successfully escape the island. But by July 25, the story changed: "Floyd Wilson, who bungled his only attempt at crime, did likewise yesterday in an effort to get off Alcatraz."

Harry S. Truman,

President of the United States of America,

To all to whom these presents shall come, Greeting:

Whereas

Floyd P. Wilson was convicted in the District Court of the United States for the District of Columbia of murder in the first degree, and on June twenty-seventh, 1947, was sentenced to death; and

Whereas the date of execution of the said Floyd P. Wilson has been deferred until August twentieth, 1948; and

Whereas it has been made to appear to me that the said Floyd P. Wilson is a fit object of Executive clemency:

Now, therefore, be it known, *that I,* **Harry S. Truman,** *President of the United States of America, in consideration of the premises, divers other good and sufficient reasons me thereunto moving, do hereby* commute the sentence of the said Floyd P. Wilson to imprisonment for life.

In testimony whereof *I have hereunto signed my name and caused the seal of the Department of Justice to be affixed.*

Done *at the City of Washington this* Third *day of* August *in the year of our Lord One Thousand Nine Hundred and* Forty-eight *and of the Independence of the United States the One Hundred and* Seventy-third.

Harry S. Truman

By the President:

Philip B. Perlman

Acting *Attorney General.*

Escape 12

Desperate Cons Fight Killer Current

Prisoners tie up guard and head for shoreline.

ESCAPE 12

DATE: September 29, 1958

LOCATION: Garbage Detail

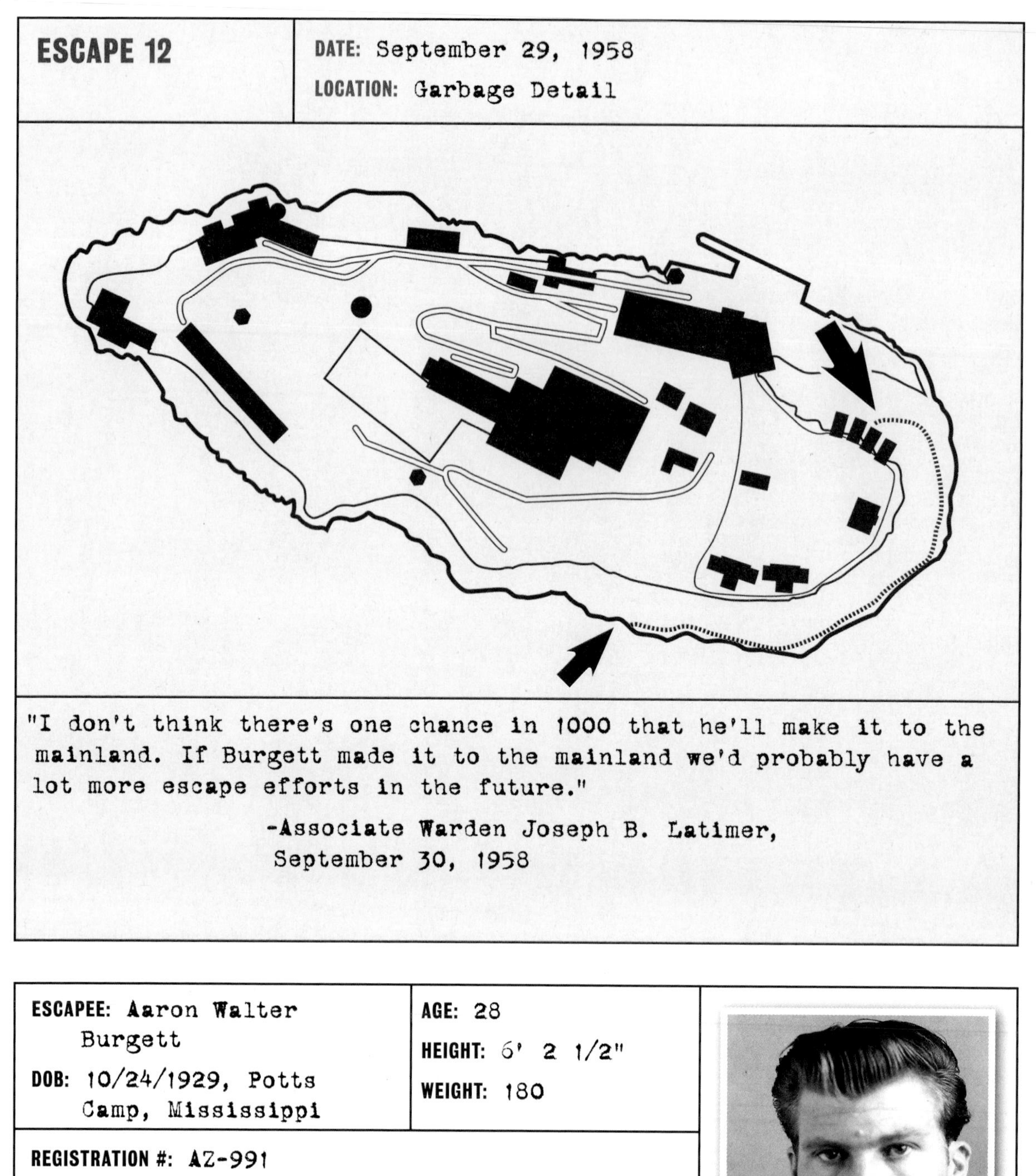

"I don't think there's one chance in 1000 that he'll make it to the mainland. If Burgett made it to the mainland we'd probably have a lot more escape efforts in the future."

-Associate Warden Joseph B. Latimer, September 30, 1958

ESCAPEE: Aaron Walter Burgett

DOB: 10/24/1929, Potts Camp, Mississippi

AGE: 28

HEIGHT: 6' 2 1/2"

WEIGHT: 180

REGISTRATION #: AZ-991

RECEIVED FROM USP LEAVENWORTH: 8/27/1952

SENTENCE: 26 years for the $15.26 armed robbery of a post office

REASON SENT TO ALCATRAZ: Length of sentence and violent escape attempt

DIED IN ATTEMPT

U. S. PENITENTIARY
ALCATRAZ
991
8 27 52

Alcatraz officials designed an elaborate set of procedures to guard inmates working outside the prison walls. But a breakdown in those procedures—and some factors beyond the guards' control—contributed to the plans of two desperate convicts. This was the last escape during which a guard's life was threatened.

Road to Alcatraz

Aaron Burgett was one of ten children raised by his widowed father. Nicknamed "Wig" because he wore his curly blonde hair long, he dropped out of school when he turned sixteen to work on the family farm. Burgett was arrested in 1945 for breaking into a candy truck and served a year at the State Training School in Booneville, Missouri, before escaping with an accomplice. He was quickly captured. After serving out his term, he continued life as a burglar. His next stint behind bars was spent in the state penitentiary in Jefferson City, Missouri. For a year, Burgett gave up his life of crime when he married Mary Frances Cauley. Although he called it the best year of his life, he was unable to find steady work, and instead, returned to the profession he knew so well. Beginning in 1952, he and two accomplices engaged in a string of violent armed robberies. The crime spree ended in a sentence to federal prison, and by the middle of that year, he was on his way to Leavenworth. En route to the prison, he made a desperate attempt to escape. Unsuccessful, he arrived at the prison covered in cuts and bruises from his struggle with the lawman in the car. At Alcatraz, Burgett was viewed as a good inmate, but described as a man easily led by others. He played the guitar, enjoyed time in the recreation yard, and was an avid reader. He also landed a job on outside garbage duty, where, along with fellow inmate Clyde Johnson, he would plot his escape.

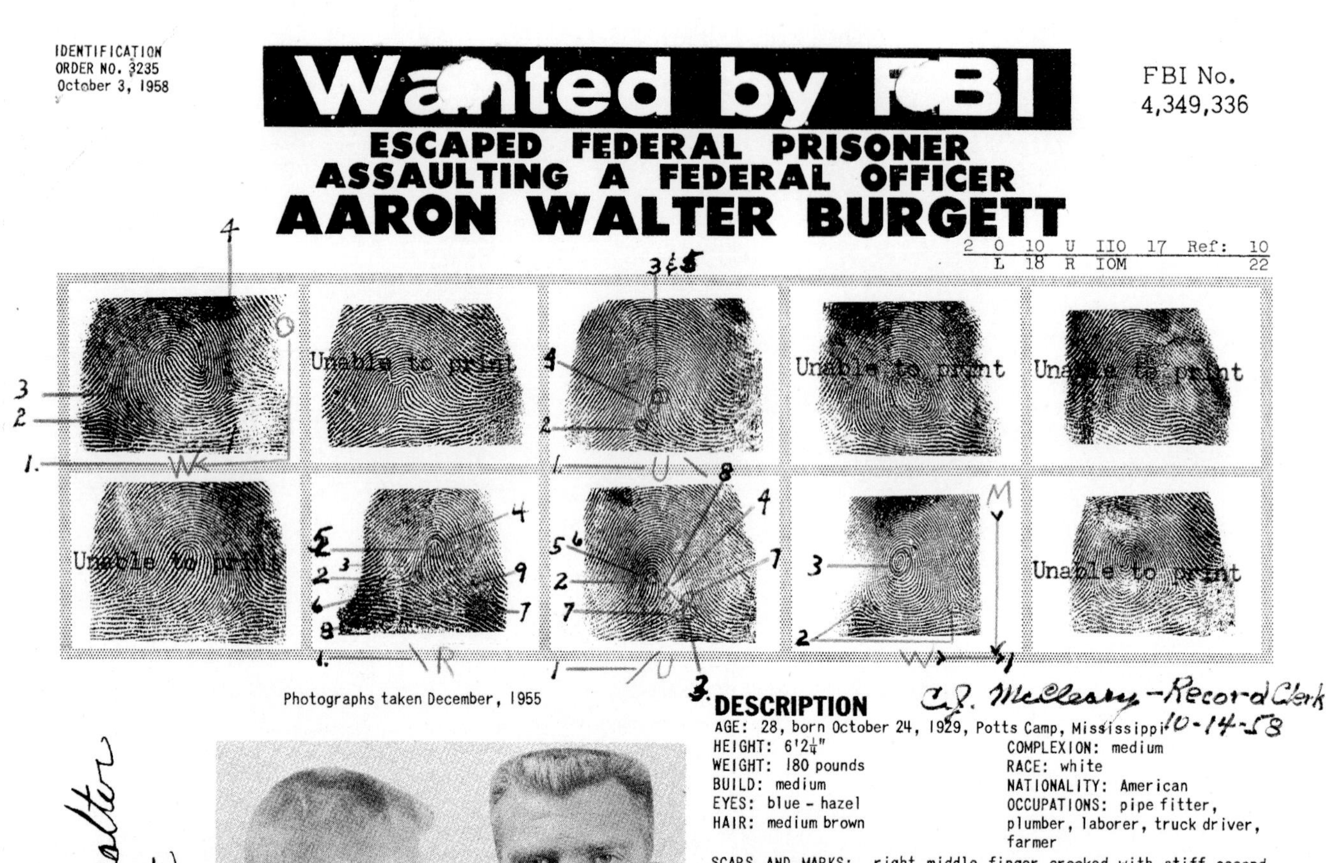

IDENTIFICATION
ORDER NO. 3235
October 3, 1958

Wanted by FBI

FBI No.
4,349,336

ESCAPED FEDERAL PRISONER
ASSAULTING A FEDERAL OFFICER
AARON WALTER BURGETT

2 0 10 U IIO 17 Ref: 10
L 18 R IOM 22

Unable to print | Unable to print | Unable to print | Unable to print | Unable to print

Photographs taken December, 1955

aaron walter Burgett

DESCRIPTION

C. J. McCleary – Record Clerk 10-14-58

AGE: 28, born October 24, 1929, Potts Camp, Mississippi
HEIGHT: 6'2¼"
WEIGHT: 180 pounds
BUILD: medium
EYES: blue - hazel
HAIR: medium brown
COMPLEXION: medium
RACE: white
NATIONALITY: American
OCCUPATIONS: pipe fitter, plumber, laborer, truck driver, farmer

SCARS AND MARKS: right middle finger crooked with stiff second joint, deep pit scars on face, red mole between eyes, tattoo on calf of right leg.

CRIMINAL RECORD

Burgett has been convicted for burglary and larceny, armed robbery and assault with a deadly weapon.

CAUTION

BURGETT USED A KNIFE TO OVERPOWER A GUARD IN ESCAPE FROM ALCATRAZ. HE PREVIOUSLY ASSAULTED CUSTODIAL OFFICER. HE SHOULD BE CONSIDERED ARMED AND EXTREMELY DANGEROUS.

A Federal complaint was filed at Oakland, California, on September 30, 1958, charging Burgett with assaulting a Federal officer. (Title 18, U. S. Code, Section 111)

IF YOU HAVE INFORMATION CONCERNING THIS PERSON, PLEASE NOTIFY ME OR CONTACT YOUR LOCAL FBI OFFICE. PHONE NUMBER IS LISTED BELOW. OTHER OFFICES ARE LISTED ON BACK.

J. Edgar Hoover
DIRECTOR
Federal Bureau of Investigation
Washington 25, D. C.

IDENTIFICATION
ORDER NO. 3235

Call San Francisco Kl 2-2155

ESCAPEE: Clyde Milton Johnson

DOB: 8/16/1918, Minneapolis Minnesota

AGE: 40

HEIGHT: 5' 10"

WEIGHT: 170

REGISTER #: AZ-864

RECEIVED FROM USP ATLANTA: 3/22/1950

SENTENCE: 40 years for bank robbery in Tennessee

REASON SENT TO ALCATRAZ: Long sentence and high escape risk

RECAPTURED

Born in Minnesota, **Clyde Johnson** grew up in Glendale, California. His father, a truck driver, died when he was two and his mother, a laundress, raised him and an older sibling. Though he was reportedly well behaved as a child and young adult, after joining the army in 1941, he deserted several times. His first crimes were grocery-store robberies, for which he was sentenced to California's San Quentin State Prison in Marin County. After his release in 1949, Johnson was involved in the armed robbery of a bank in Memphis, Tennessee. He and his accomplice made off with $43,662, but were soon apprehended. While awaiting extradition, the stick-up artist escaped from the twenty-one-story Dade County Jail in Miami, Florida; arrested again, he fired on FBI agents before his capture. He landed at the federal penitentiary in Atlanta, then Leavenworth, and finally, in 1950, was transferred to Alcatraz. One of the FBI's "Ten Most Wanted Fugitives" had reached the end of the line.

The Plan

Prison officials speculated that Burgett and Johnson had been planning their escape for some time. They maintained good conduct records, which allowed them to be assigned to the garbage detail outside the prison walls. This gave them plenty of time to survey the grounds and determine where to subdue a guard without fear of detection. After assembling the tools they needed—a kitchen paring knife, plastic bags, extra clothes, sections of raincoats, plywood, and electrician's tape—they waited out the days until the time changed from daylight savings to standard, hoping the early darkness would help conceal their escape. Finally, they monitored the job rotations of the guards until a new, less-experienced

guard was assigned to their detail. Although Johnson claimed they did not factor fog into their plans, there was no question it aided them. Their goal was to overpower the guard; slip into the water; and, using handmade water wings and fins, swim to freedom.

Sign at the beach.

The Escape

As they rolled out their plan, luck seemed to be on their side. A lapse in one of the prison's most routine actions, the prisoner count, spurred them on. Every time a boat left the island, inmates on outside details had to be accounted for by one of the tower or control-room guards. On the day of the escape attempt, one of the guards mistakenly thought the two men working the garbage detail were accounted for, which gave the escapees an unanticipated and most fortunate hour's head start. As if this weren't enough of a break, the new officer who had been assigned to the garbage detail didn't have a thorough understanding of his post. Burgett and Johnson were quick to take advantage of the situation.

Johnson entered the water along the western shoreline.

All appeared normal on the island when, at 3:45 PM, a heavy fog rolled in and orders were given to bring all the crews in early. However, when a count was taken and the garbage crew and Officer Miller were determined to be missing, Associate Warden Latimer ordered the escape alarm sounded. A search party was swiftly dispatched to the area, and the Coast Guard was called in. By 4:30, Miller was found tied to a tree with his mouth thoroughly taped, and at 4:45, a crewman on a Coast Guard boat spotted Johnson up to his waist in water on the western side of the island, too scared to swim. Blue with cold, the convict was hurried to the warden's office for questioning by the FBI. Burgett remained missing.

Johnson laid out the details of the escape attempt in a formal interview with Associate Warden Joseph Latimer. According to Latimer,

> Johnson said that the officer, Harold Miller, made his check call at 2:30 PM from the vicinity of the Fog Horn Station. He said that he, Miller, and Burgett proceeded to the gate by the Associate Warden's house and they convinced Miller that they should go into this area and clean the roadway and drainage outlets. He claims they swept and picked up considerable trash and then suggested to Miller that they carry the trash over to the stone wall and dump it down the face of the cliff. He says that they also told Miller that it was part of their duty to keep the cactus trimmed along the pathway leading from the gate to the beach facing Fisherman's Wharf and they suggested looking this over to see if it needed trimming.

INEXPERIENCE TRIPS UP GUARD

"They jumped me with a knife," said Guard Harold Miller, "and told me I'd be all right if I was good." Alcatraz guards were considered to be the best in the federal system. Trained in everything from judo and firearms to psychology, they were expected to enforce the rules and regulations to the letter. But from the time the prison opened in 1934, turnover among prison guards was high. In 1938, Warden Johnston reported an 18 percent annual turnover; by the end of World War II, that number was 35 percent. Dangerous convicts, escape attempts, and the infamous Battle of Alcatraz took their toll; by the 1950s, it was getting difficult to recruit guards to work on Alcatraz. Officer Arthur Dollison reported that at times, one-third of the officers had less than a year of prison experience. "They were as green as grass," said Captain Bergen, "and the prisoners have hundreds of years of experience."

Guard Harold Miller had been a casket-maker before becoming a prison guard; he

Continued next page

From previous page

was twenty years old when he reported to duty on Alcatraz. After ten months, he was assigned to garbage detail, one of the more dangerous assignments for the correctional staff. There, inmates worked outside the prison walls, moved around the island, and had access to sharp gardening tools. Miller had been assigned to the garbage detail for only four days before the breakout attempt. Burgett and Johnson, who had worked there for nearly six months, had plenty of time to plan their escape.

On the day of the escape, September 29, Officer Miller —in violation of his duties —failed to keep the two convicts in view of the guard tower for the afternoon head count, and naively accompanied them down a path where they could subdue him without being observed by anyone on the island. Officer Miller said he hadn't read his orders too thoroughly and wasn't sure what he should allow the prisoners to do. However, he said the experience had not deterred him from continuing as a guard.

As they were returning along the path toward the gate, Burgett was in the lead, followed by Miller, with Johnson coming up the rear. Johnson says that at a point about thirty feet from the gate they pulled a knife on Miller and taped his hands and mouth. They then guided Miller down the hill to the vicinity of the large wooden warning sign on the beach where they tied Miller to a tree. Johnson states that the two of them then went westward toward the cement steps at the foot of the pathway. At this point, they observed a boat approaching near the island. They became alarmed and headed back toward the place where they had left Miller. They examined Miller's bindings to make sure he was suffering no ill effects and had not been able to loosen them.

Johnson claims that when they left Miller the second time, he and Burgett parted company. He says he continued westward and finally removed a plastic bag from underneath his sweatshirt where he had been carrying it folded. He says he then inflated this bag to the best of his ability and fastened the opening securely. He says the bag was some 2' x 3" in size. Johnson claims that up to this point he had intended to hide out until dark but after inflating the bag, he decided to try immediately. When he stepped into the water he states that "the bag was torn from my hands and I lost not only the bag but just about everything I had, including my dental plate." He claims that at

Bay Balks Convict's Break for Freedom

At left, Deputy Coroner Ken Kindred is holding the plastic bag which convict Aaron Burgett inflated to serve as water wings in his futile attempt to escape from Alcatraz. On floor are books of paper matches, roll of friction tape, extra shoelaces and bits of cloth taken from water logged trousers of dead convict. On table are articles of clothing, including Burgett's shoes with swim fin attached to one of them. Below is closeup of the shoes showing broken home made plywood swim fin which was attached to the convict's left shoe with friction tape and piece of wire.

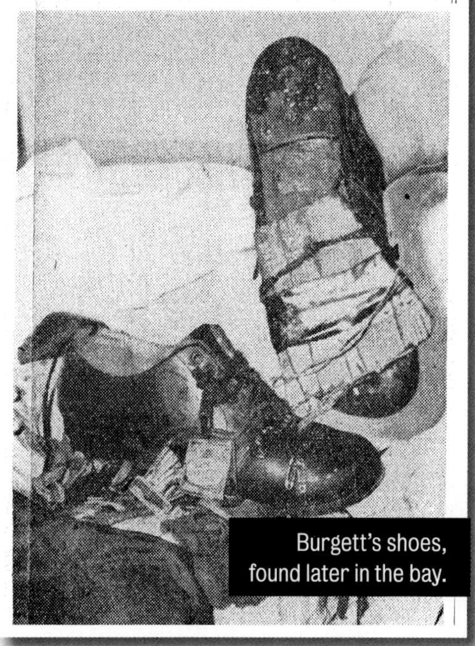

Burgett's shoes, found later in the bay.

this time he gave up all hope of escaping, as he did not think it possible to escape by swimming or even floating in the cold water. Johnson also claims that inmate Burgett changed his mind several times; one time he would argue that they should try to escape into the water as quickly as possible; at another time he would feel they should wait until dark before getting off the island.

The Aftermath

Burgett had disappeared. For ten days, special patrols combed every inch of the island. Finally, Warden Madigan called them off. Thirteen days after the escape attempt, Burgett's partially decomposed body was taken from San Francisco Bay after a tower guard spotted it floating about one hundred yards off the east end of the island. The belt on the body was stenciled "991," Burgett's number. In a pocket was the thin, sharp knife Burgett had used to seize Miller. Plastic tape was secured to the soles of his shoes, holding what remained of a pair of homemade wooden fins. Attached to his belt was a plastic bag "water wing." Burgett's was the only body to be recovered from the bay in the penitentiary's history.

San Francisco's newspapers covered the escape attempt for almost two weeks. In a letter to the Bureau of Prisons director, Warden Madigan wrote, "Copies of the four San Francisco papers for the week are being sent to you and even though they side-tracked the war in Formosa with Alcatraz headlines, they treated us fairly well. We are also enclosing a clipping from the San Francisco newspaper which describes a swim made by Jack LaLanne, a San Francisco swimmer . . . proving quite conclusively that it is very difficult to swim away from the island."

Escape 13

Brilliant Escape Artists Vanish Without a Trace

Dummy heads delay discovery.

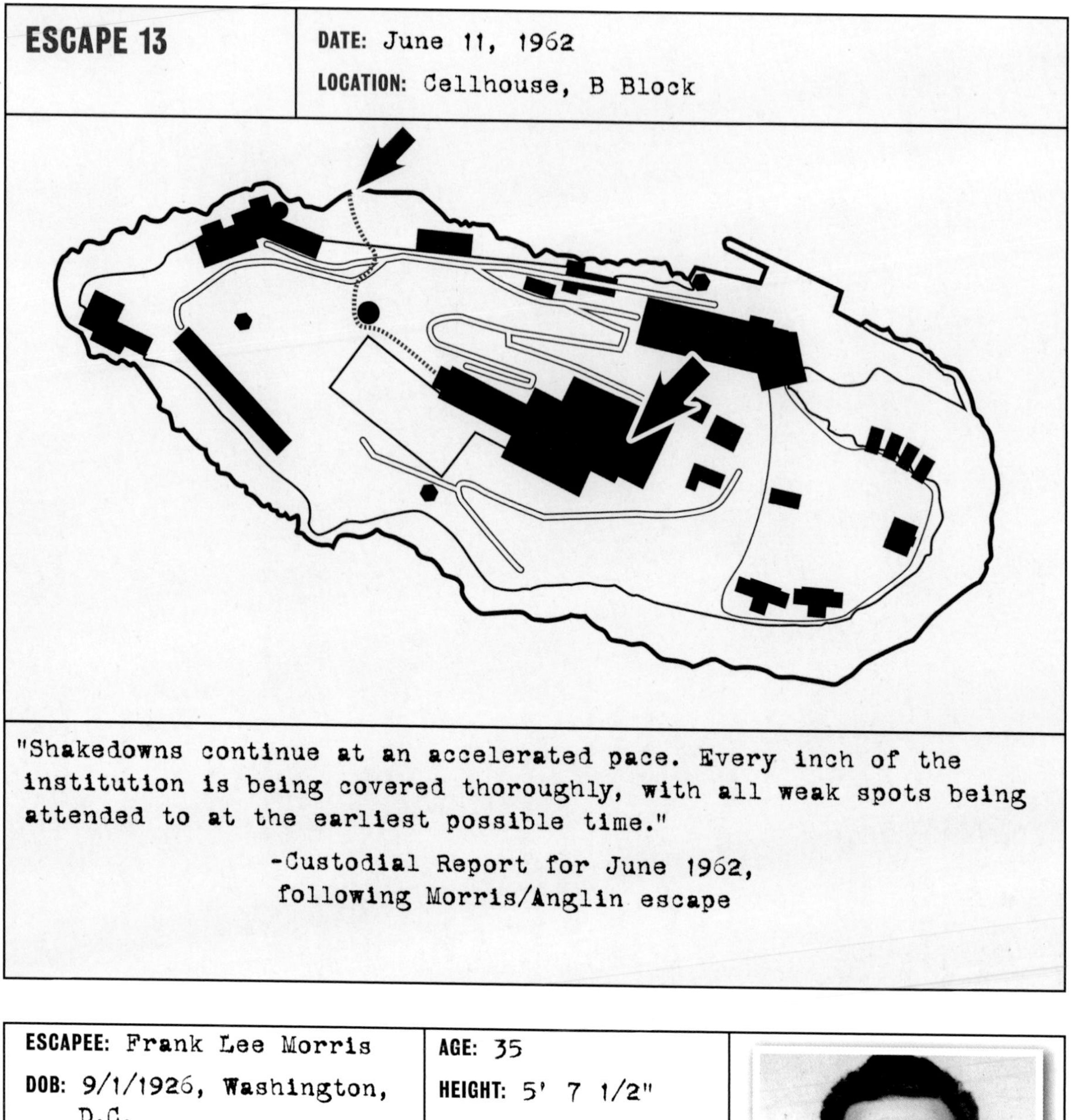

ESCAPE 13

DATE: June 11, 1962

LOCATION: Cellhouse, B Block

"Shakedowns continue at an accelerated pace. Every inch of the institution is being covered thoroughly, with all weak spots being attended to at the earliest possible time."

-Custodial Report for June 1962, following Morris/Anglin escape

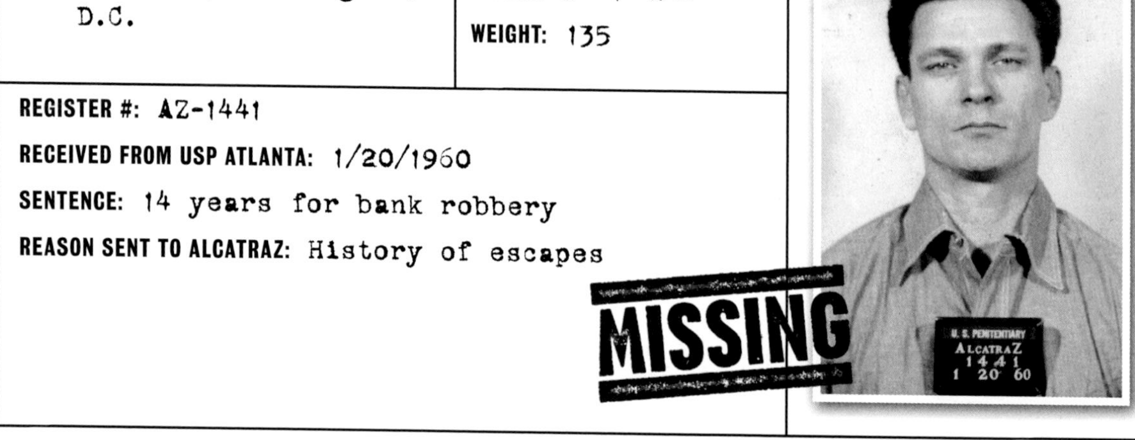

ESCAPEE: Frank Lee Morris

DOB: 9/1/1926, Washington, D.C.

AGE: 35

HEIGHT: 5' 7 1/2"

WEIGHT: 135

REGISTER #: AZ-1441

RECEIVED FROM USP ATLANTA: 1/20/1960

SENTENCE: 14 years for bank robbery

REASON SENT TO ALCATRAZ: History of escapes

Did they make it, or did they die trying? In the most famous and complicated escape attempt on the Rock, Frank Morris and the Anglin brothers burrowed out of their cells and fled from the prison stronghold into the cold bay waters. Hollywood's most famous portrayal of the event—*Escape from Alcatraz*—keeps the speculation alive.

Road to Alcatraz

Abandoned at birth, **Frank Morris** spent his childhood in a series of foster homes and his teen years on the wrong side of the law. Arrested for burglary at thirteen, by his late teens, Morris had been picked up for crimes ranging from narcotics possession to armed robbery. He was reported to have "superior intelligence" (an IQ of 133) and he definitely had a special talent for escaping from prisons—he attempted to break out of every institution that held him. During a seven-year sentence at the state prison in Raiford, Florida, he escaped five times. He was short and lean, with a star tattooed on his forehead, the number 13 tattooed on his finger, and a haunted look in his eyes. As an adult, Morris served time in five state prisons and ended up at USP Atlanta for robbing a Louisiana bank. On January 20,1960, Morris was sent to the Rock for "closer custody." There, he reconnected with some old friends from USP Atlanta, brothers Clarence and John Anglin.

The **Anglin brothers** grew up in Florida farm country in a family of fourteen children. Every summer, they traveled north to pick cherries, and the boys learned to swim in the icy waters of Lake Michigan. They often played hooky from school; Clarence made it through fifth grade, and John, through third. The boys began getting into trouble at a young age, and youthful mischievousness had turned into petty crime by the time they were teenagers. By the 1950s, the two young men, along with brother Alfred, were robbing banks, being charged as adults, and spending time in a variety of state prisons, where they were known as escape artists. After managing to break out of the Florida State Penitentiary in 1958, the brothers robbed the Bank of Columbia in Alabama. Within four days, the FBI had tracked them down in Ohio. This time, they were sent to the federal penitentiary in Atlanta (where they first met Morris and West), and not long thereafter, were transferred to Leavenworth due to their reputations for escape. One of Clarence's more memorable plots at Leavenworth involved hiding John among loaves of bread in a bakery truck. Like Morris, the bank-robbing duo landed at Alcatraz in the early 1960s. John, known as J.W., was described as bumbling, but with a certain charm. His younger brother was smarter and more aggressive. Both were loudmouthed, with a penchant for bragging about

ESCAPEE: John Anglin
DOB: 5/2/1930, Donalsonville, Georgia
AGE: 32
HEIGHT: 5' 10"
WEIGHT: 140
REGISTER #: AZ-1476
RECEIVED FROM USP LEAVENWORTH: 10/22/1960
SENTENCE: 10 years for bank robbery
REASON SENT TO ALCATRAZ: History of escape attempts

MISSING

U. S. PENITENTIARY
ALCATRAZ
1476
10 24 60

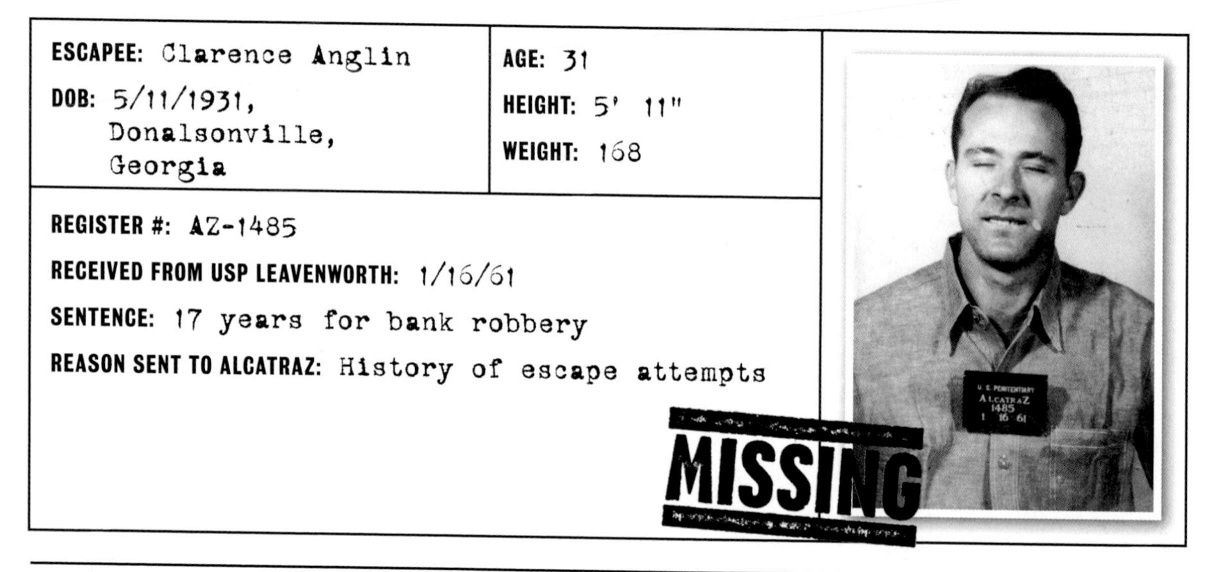
ESCAPEE: Clarence Anglin
DOB: 5/11/1931, Donalsonville, Georgia
AGE: 31
HEIGHT: 5' 11"
WEIGHT: 168
REGISTER #: AZ-1485
RECEIVED FROM USP LEAVENWORTH: 1/16/61
SENTENCE: 17 years for bank robbery
REASON SENT TO ALCATRAZ: History of escape attempts

MISSING

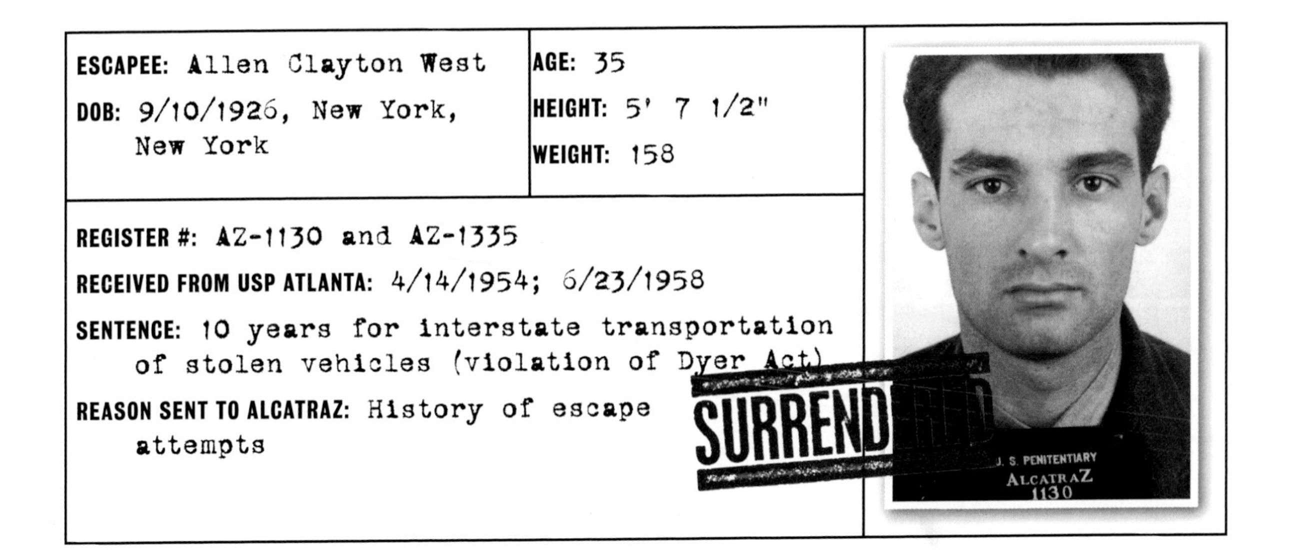

ESCAPEE: Allen Clayton West
DOB: 9/10/1926, New York, New York
AGE: 35
HEIGHT: 5' 7 1/2"
WEIGHT: 158
REGISTER #: AZ-1130 and AZ-1335
RECEIVED FROM USP ATLANTA: 4/14/1954; 6/23/1958
SENTENCE: 10 years for interstate transportation of stolen vehicles (violation of Dyer Act)
REASON SENT TO ALCATRAZ: History of escape attempts

their achievements, large and small. Throughout their criminal careers, they had been reckless and incompetent, a bad combination. A former girlfriend of John's said, "They weren't bad guys, they were just dirt poor."

Allen West was hot-headed and arrogant. Arrested more than twenty times for car theft and breaking and entering, he spent time in the federal penitentiary at Atlanta, where he met Morris and the Anglin brothers. He was sent to Alcatraz in 1954 and again in 1958. On the Rock, he provoked arguments and helped fuel racial tensions among prisoners; most cons steered clear of him. Like Morris and the Anglins, West had a history of escape attempts. Some believe West was actually the ringleader in the 1962 plot. Others disagree, noting that Morris had orchestrated similar attempts in the past. In either event, West was an active conspirator, helping with the elaborate preparations for the breakout.

Officer Orin T. Maybee photographs the loose ventilator cap on the cellhouse roof.

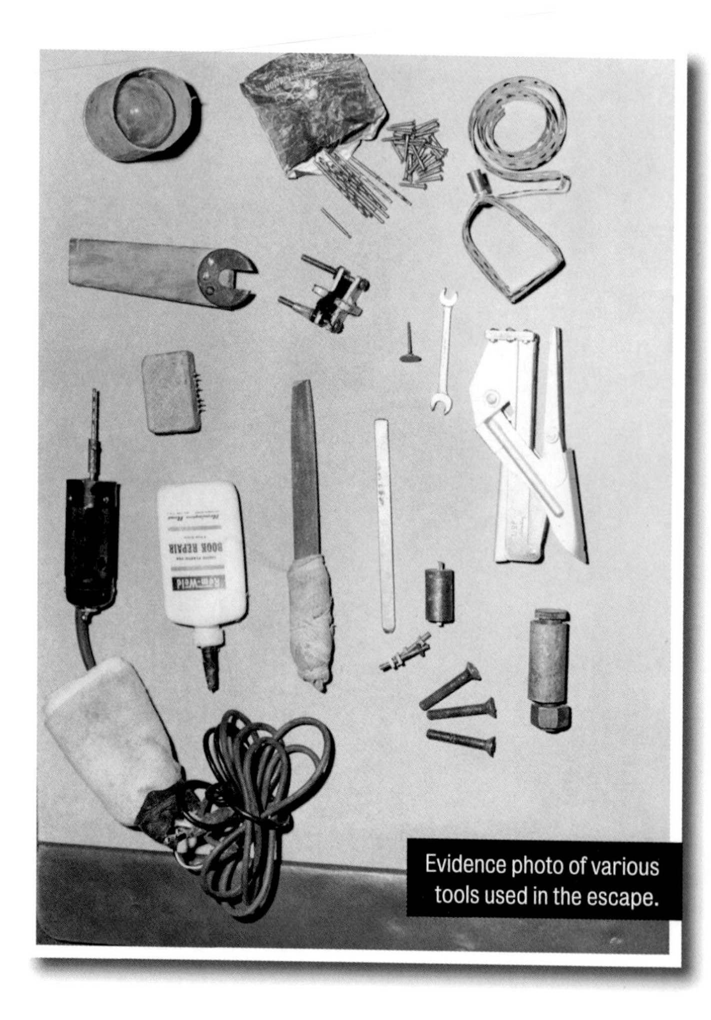

Evidence photo of various tools used in the escape.

The Plan

Frank Morris, John and Clarence Anglin, and Allen West arrived at Alcatraz at different times, but from the moment each set foot on the island, they all had the same goal: getting off the Rock. Their plan rested on a single chink in the Alcatraz armor, which had been discovered by West while on cleaning detail: a ventilator cap at the top of the cellhouse that had not been cemented shut. This would give them access to the roof. After enlarging the air vents at the back of their cells, the men planned to enter the narrow utility corridor that ran behind all their cells, climb the pipes to the top of the three-tier cell block, and exit through the vent to the prison's roof. From there, they would slide down a sturdy drain pipe to the ground, then head for the shoreline and paddle to freedom on a makeshift raft. Their goal was to make their way to Angel Island, then, after resting, swim to Marin. Once they made land, they would steal a car, rob a clothing store, and take off in separate directions.

The details were complicated and the gear required was extensive. Fashioning tools from reinforced spoons, they slowly chipped away at the wall around the vents.* Removable sections of plaster were painted to look like the surrounding wall area and fake grilles made from cardboard covered the holes. They ingeniously constructed a set of crude but lifelike heads using materials found

---

* There is some controversy around this; many years later, a former correctional officer and a former prisoner each commented that despite Alcatraz's age, its walls couldn't be cut through with spoons.

around the prison and covertly passed along to them by other inmates: soap chips, concrete, plaster, glue, flesh-tone paint from prison art kits, and real hair clippings smuggled from the barber shop. These heads would serve as decoys during the guards' nightly counts. The Anglin brothers were assigned to adjoining cells; Morris and West were in adjoining cells four doors down. While other prisoners read, played music (sometimes loudly, to cover the sounds of digging), or slept, the four desperados worked—and watched out for one another—almost four hours each night for months on end.

As part of the plan, West landed a job cleaning and painting the space above the top tier of cells. He convinced one of the guards that he needed to hang blankets around his work area to prevent debris from falling into the cells. Hidden by the blankets, the four men set up a workshop on a platform above the cellblock and began the next stage of the escape project. Using instructions they found in an issue of *Popular Mechanics*, they designed a raft from about fifty prison-issued rubber raincoats, most of which were stolen. To go with it, they built life preservers and plywood paddles. Several years previously, inmates had been allowed to have instruments, so Morris ordered a concertina (a small accordion-like instrument) and modified it so it could be used as a bellows to inflate the raft.

The men took turns climbing through their cell vents and up the utility chase

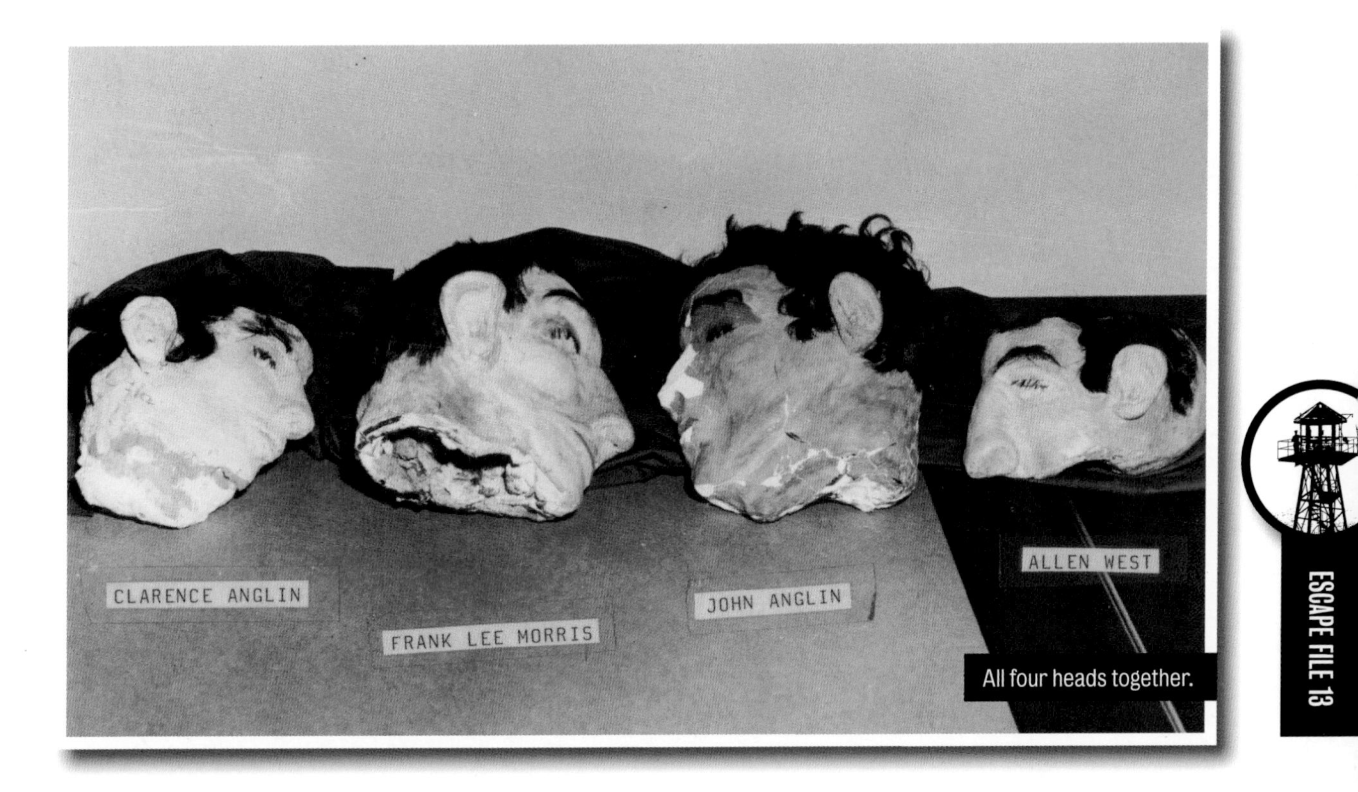

All four heads together.

Adm. Form No. 62
(Rev. 11-1958)

RECORD OF GOOD TIME FORFEITURE

U. S. Penitentiary
Alcatraz, California
(Institution)

Name: ANGLIN, John William   No. 1476-AZ   Date hearing June 25, 1962

Good time allowance 1200 days   Good time earned to date of violation: 206 days SGT and 8 days EGT

Statement of Violation: ESCAPE: Inmate John William Anglin #1476-AZ is charged with breaking out of the rear of his cell (B-150) and escape from Alcatraz Island. He was discovered missing at about 7:18 a. m. June 12, 1962 by this officer, while making a count. A plaster head was found in his bed.

****

Inmate was tried in absentia. It was unanimously recommended by the Board that this inmate forfeit all SGT and EGT up to date of the offense.

Officer reporting violation: Lawrence I. Bartlett

Penalty recommended by Good Time Forfeiture Board:

(1) Forfeiture of 214 days Good Time — A. M. Dollison, Associate Warden, Chairman

(2) Forfeiture of 214 days Good Time — T. D. Bradley, Captain, Member

(3) Forfeiture of 214 days Good Time — J. W. Casey, Chief, M.T.A., Member

I hereby impose the following penalty on the above-named prisoner: Forfeiture of 206 days Statutory Good Time and 8 days Earned Good Time, a total of 214 days.

O. G. Blackwell
Warden-Superintendent

Date 7/2/62

FPI—LK—12-28-59—9M—7582

Senior Officer Howard Waldron in Frank Morris's cell looking at the point of escape.

to work on dislodging the ventilator cap. West swiped a motor from a vacuum cleaner and made a motorized drill, but it turned out to be noisy and too weak to loosen the rivets holding the rooftop ventilator in place. Finally, they managed to break through the vent's fastenings with an abrasive cord. One of the men scored the crowbar they needed to spread the bar across the ventilator. After seven months, the clever scheme would be put to the test.

The Escape

Just after lights-out on June 11, the prisoners made their break. Morris and the Anglins retrieved the dummy heads from their hiding places atop the cellblock; placed them in the beds; collected the raft, accessories, and a number of possessions; then left their cells for the last time. For Allen West, the nightmare was just beginning. He'd recently cemented the fake cardboard grill in place because it had been slipping and he was afraid it

In the utility corridor, an officer inspects the opening from one of the cells.

ESCAPE FILE 13

The FBI pursued leads for decades before closing the files.

would be discovered. As the others were scurrying up the utility chase, West couldn't get out of his cell. He furiously chipped at the cement, trying to rip off the vent grill. When he finally dislodged it and got to the roof, his accomplices were gone.

The Aftermath

At 7:15 the next morning, guards made their routine head count. Each prisoner was supposed to stand at the front of his cell while the guard checked off his name off the list. Morris, it seemed, still asleep; the Anglins too appeared to be in bed. Guards unlocked the cells to rouse them. The officer nudged Morris's head, and jumped back in shock when it rolled onto the floor. Two more dummy heads were found in John and Clarence Anglin's cells.

The prison went into immediate lockdown and guards swarmed through the cellhouse. The FBI sped to the island with bloodhounds, which tracked the inmates' scent to the shoreline. In the meantime, Alcatraz officials discovered the enlarged opening in the four men's cells. When questioned, West gave the FBI details of the plan and took credit for planning most of it.

The investigation was far-flung and extensive, but no signs of Morris or the Anglin brothers were ever found. No car thefts or clothing-store robberies were reported locally in the days following the breakout, and the men did not seem to have had any friends or contacts in San Francisco who could have assisted them with their escape. More than two hundred soldiers scoured Angel Island, and the FBI poured three hundred agents into the search. Not an inch of land on Alcatraz or Angel Island went unexamined.

The rec yard wall catwalk was among the vantage points used by guards to scan the bay.

The first tangible clue turned up a few days later. A watertight plastic bag scooped out of the bay contained dozens of snapshots, a receipt for a $10 money order made out to Clarence Anglin, and a list of names and addresses. Then an oar was found floating off Angel Island. The next piece of evidence washed up on a Marin beach. It was a yard of black polyethylene with a series of knots tied in it as if an attempt had been made to use it as a water wing. Another makeshift lifejacket, covered in bloodstains, was found about fifty yards east of the Alcatraz dock. On June 20, a bundle of hatch-covered planks, lashed together by a rope, turned up on the shores of Sausalito. A month later, a Norwegian freighter spotted a body clad in denim floating twenty miles northwest Golden Gate Bridge but failed to report the discovery for another three months. Although authorities suspected that it was that of one of the three escapees, it had deteriorated too much to be identified.

The inmates' bodies were never recovered and the escapees never contacted their families. For years, the FBI followed up leads. Finally, in 1979, the case was officially closed and the three were recorded as missing and presumed drowned. Warden Olin Blackwell blamed the escape on the fact that the prison was deteriorating, but there was no question that lax security also contributed to the greatest escape every seen on the Rock.

ALCATRAZ AND HOLLYWOOD

Hollywood has invoked Alcatraz in movie after movie, using the island's atmosphere and location to enhance its stories and sell tickets. For example, the earliest Alcatraz-themed movie, *Alcatraz Island*, premiered in 1937 and opened with this line: "America's penal fortress, grim and mysterious as its name—where cold steel and rushing tides protect civilization from its enemies." Moviegoers may have thought they were getting a look inside the infamous prison, but it was the mid-1960s before film crews were allowed on the island; *Point Blank* (1967) was the first to use it for a few of its location shots. The most recent movie to be made there, *The Rock* (1996), was shot in almost every area of the island, both interior and exterior. In return for this use, the studio worked with the National Park Service to upgrade and repair many of Alcatraz's landmark features.

News of the escape shocked the nation. "Out of Alcatraz by a Spoon," the headlines blared. Without the bodies of the escapees, the legend of their daring run remained alive. West, the left-behind conspirator, was among the last prisoners to be transferred from Alcatraz when it closed in 1963 and served time in Georgia and Florida prisons. After fatally stabbing another prisoner, he was sentenced to life and in 1978, died in prison of peritonitis.

Seventeen years after the incident, Clint Eastwood starred as Frank Morris in the film classic, *Escape from Alcatraz*, and a 2003 episode of Discovery Channel's *MythBusters* indicated that such an escape was possible. In November 2005, the story of the escape was rebroadcast on *America's Most Wanted*. Each year, more than one million people visit Alcatraz for a firsthand look at the infamous cells where the escape began.

STANLEY MOSK
ATTORNEY GENERAL

STATE OF CALIFORNIA

A. L. Coffey
CHIEF OF BUREAU

BUREAU OF CRIMINAL IDENTIFICATION AND INVESTIGATION

Department of Justice

P. O. BOX 1859, SACRAMENTO 9

July 31, 1962

James V. Bennett, Director
United States Department of Justice
Bureau of Prisons
Washington 25, D. C.

Dear Mr. Bennett:

Shortly after the recent escape of three prisoners from Alcatraz Prison, efforts were immediately made to obtain fingerprints of the three escapees so that positive identification could be had in connection with wanted notices in the event any one of the escapees were arrested in California for misdemeanor charges.

It was learned that the only fingerprint cards for these subjects were located at Alcatraz Prison. They had only one copy of fingerprints for each escapee and no facilities for copying and their rules did not permit them to release the fingerprint cards for duplication in San Francisco. We received the desired sets of prints after a delay of one week.

Because of the above incident and in the best interests of law enforcement in the State of California, I have been prompted to suggest that if possible arrangements be made to furnish this Bureau with fingerprints of inmates of Federal prisons within the State of California.

If it is possible for you to accede to our request and comply with this suggestion, we would greatly appreciate it.

Very truly yours,

A L Coffey

A. L. COFFEY
Chief of Bureau

Dick Heaney — This is comparable with the inquiry rec'd from State Police in Pennsylvania re: Lewisburg inmate. Pls. check prior corresp. — Believe we should ask LC for their comment. Tell Coffey that we are looking into this. J

Escape 14

Racing Currents Carry Convict to Golden Gate

Coast Guard cutters search the foggy nighttime bay.

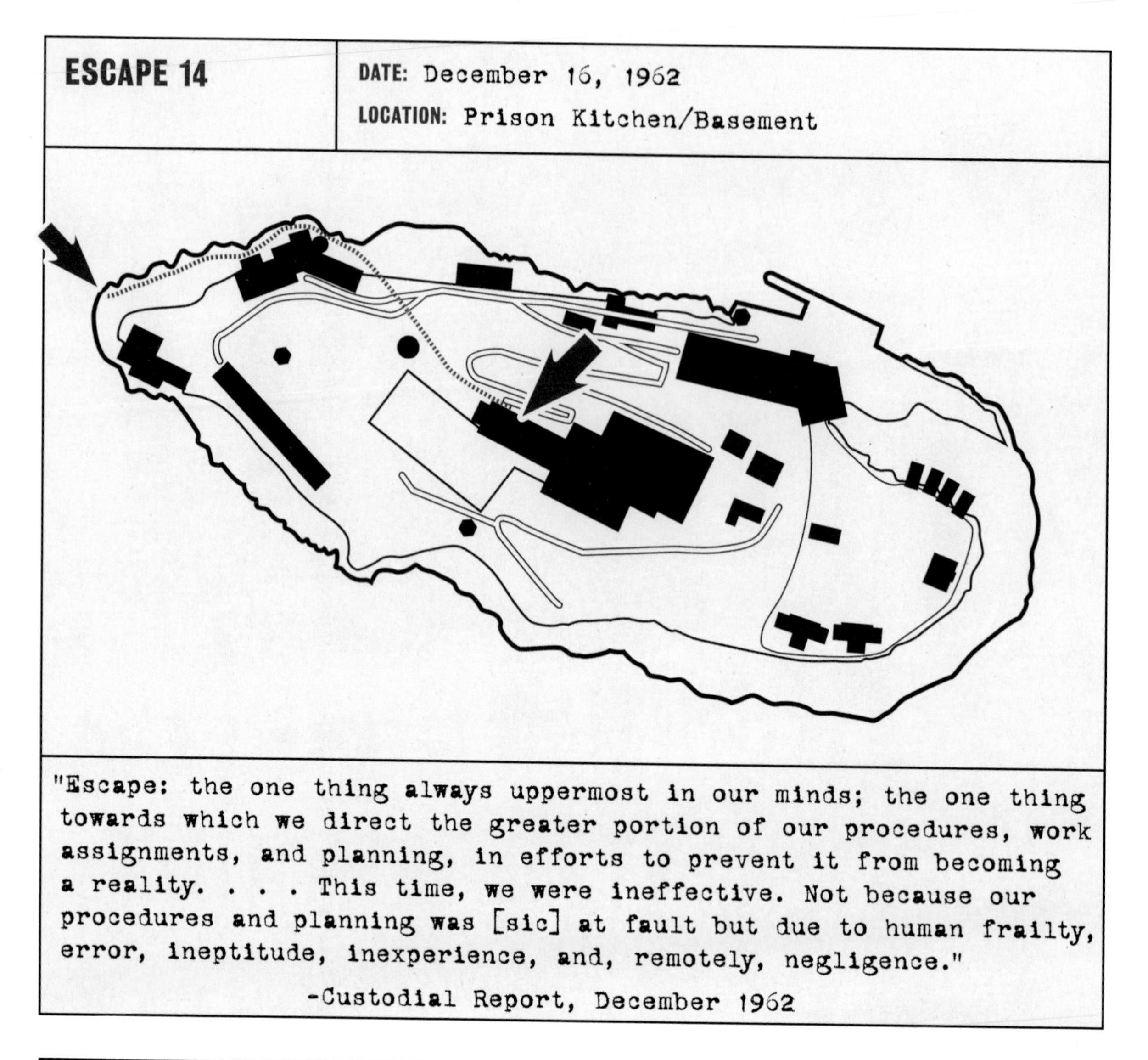

ESCAPE 14

DATE: December 16, 1962

LOCATION: Prison Kitchen/Basement

"Escape: the one thing always uppermost in our minds; the one thing towards which we direct the greater portion of our procedures, work assignments, and planning, in efforts to prevent it from becoming a reality. . . . This time, we were ineffective. Not because our procedures and planning was [sic] at fault but due to human frailty, error, ineptitude, inexperience, and, remotely, negligence."

-Custodial Report, December 1962

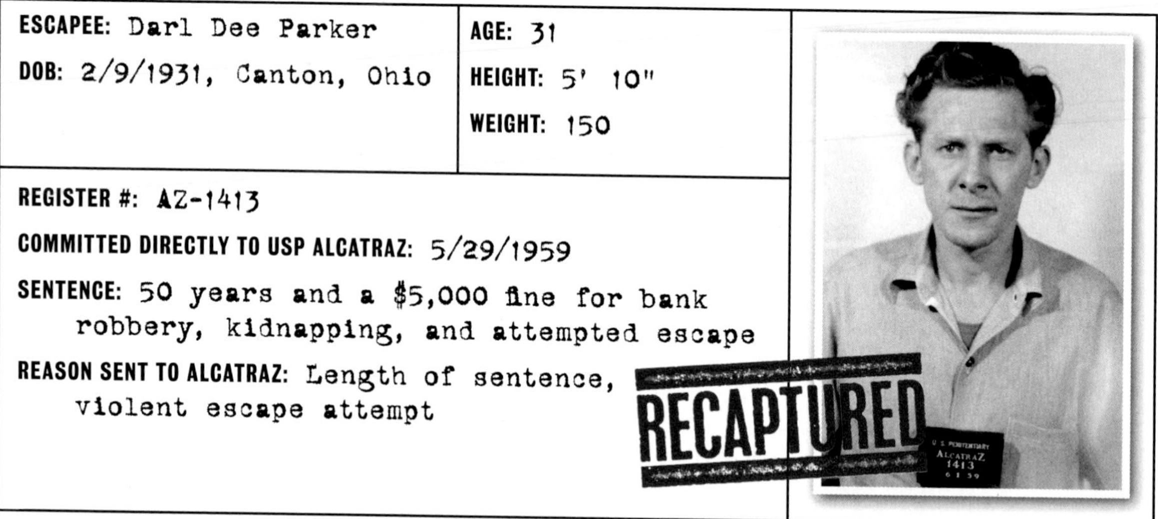

ESCAPEE: Darl Dee Parker

DOB: 2/9/1931, Canton, Ohio

AGE: 31

HEIGHT: 5' 10"

WEIGHT: 150

REGISTER #: AZ-1413

COMMITTED DIRECTLY TO USP ALCATRAZ: 5/29/1959

SENTENCE: 50 years and a $5,000 fine for bank robbery, kidnapping, and attempted escape

REASON SENT TO ALCATRAZ: Length of sentence, violent escape attempt

One determined inmate took on the cold, fast currents that had dragged many to their deaths and survived. The last break, made just months before the prison shut its doors, destroyed once and for all the myth that Alcatraz was escape-proof, and that the bay was an uncrossable boundary.

Road to Alcatraz

Darl Dee Parker was one of eight children, high-strung and quick-tempered from the start. He wasted no time getting into trouble. At age thirteen, he was charged with burglary and sent to a juvenile lockup; his criminal record continued to grow. In 1957, he masterminded a bank heist in Indiana. Disguising himself with black hair dye and theatrical greasepaint, Parker wielded a .357 Magnum revolver, stole more than $50,000, and threatened to take hostages and kill them. He was charged with robbery and committed to the Allen County Jail in Fort Wayne. The following year, he staged a violent escape, using saw blades and a pistol he had smuggled in. Cutting through the bolt on his cell door, he pulled the gun on the guard who brought him lunch and took his uniform. He then forced a dispatcher to unlock the jail's outside door and fled. Taking a mail carrier hostage, he was driven out of the Fort Wayne area. When they ran into a roadblock, a gun battle followed, during which Parker was shot in the hip and returned to jail only five hours after his bid for freedom began. Sentenced to fifty years in a federal penitentiary, he was committed directly to Alcatraz. In view of the long sentence, Parker, who had been married since 1952, advised his wife to obtain a divorce. Alcatraz officials described Parker as very moody and dangerous, and noted that other inmates seemed to avoid him. Prior to his escape attempt, he was cited for possessing home-brew, self-mutilation, and exploding a makeshift bomb in his cell.

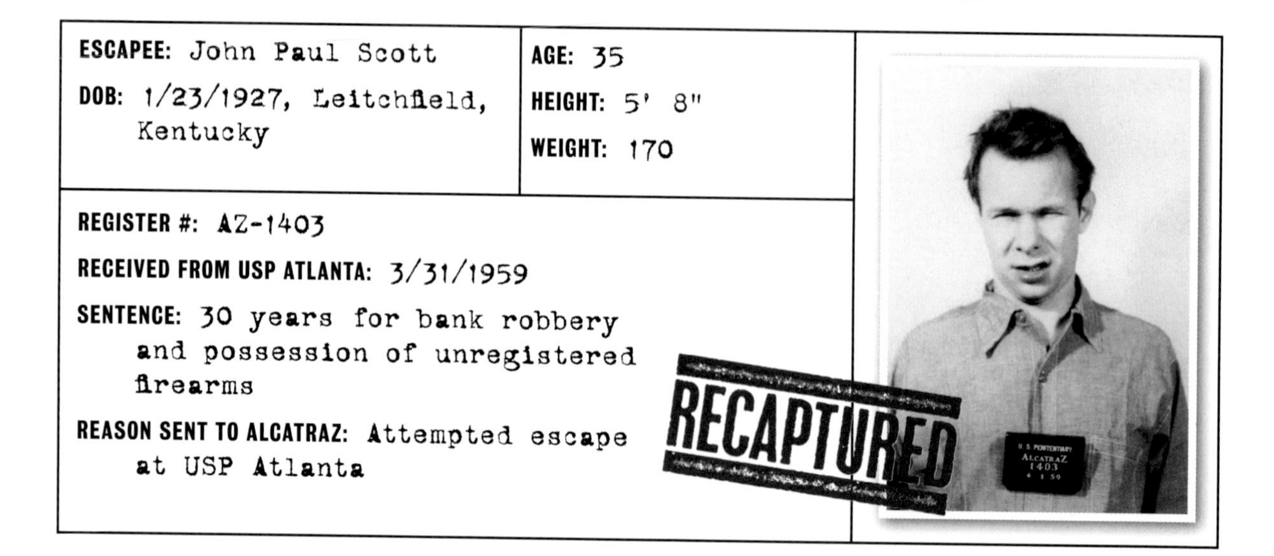

ESCAPEE: John Paul Scott

DOB: 1/23/1927, Leitchfield, Kentucky

AGE: 35

HEIGHT: 5' 8"

WEIGHT: 170

REGISTER #: AZ-1403

RECEIVED FROM USP ATLANTA: 3/31/1959

SENTENCE: 30 years for bank robbery and possession of unregistered firearms

REASON SENT TO ALCATRAZ: Attempted escape at USP Atlanta

RECAPTURED

John Paul Scott, the son of a postmaster, had an uneventful childhood. After graduating from high school in 1944, he went on to college, completing courses at the University of Kentucky, Western State Teachers College, the University of Georgia, and Georgia State University. His criminal career began in 1949 and ended with the robbery of the Farmers and Traders Bank of Campton, Kentucky, in 1957, using guns stolen from the nearby National Guard armory. During the robbery, one officer was shot in the legs and Scott was found two days later, suffering from gunshot wounds to the mouth and arm. Sent to the federal pen in Atlanta, he was then transferred to Alcatraz two years later after he and three other inmates attempted to escape from a window in the hospital surgery room. On Alcatraz, officials considered him dependable, with a good attitude and clean work record. Inmates viewed him as meek, quiet, and non-threatening—an unlikely candidate to make a break.

The Plan

Scott began planning his escape more than a year in advance, recruiting other inmates to help him. According to prison reports, relays of prisoners quietly sawed away at a barred window four feet wide and six feet high in the basement of the kitchen—most likely with a serrated spatula and a sharp grease scraper used by the fry cooks. Moist string dipped in an abrasive kitchen cleanser may also have

Sections of steel bar cut from escape window.

been used. The window was out of sight of the guard towers and ten feet above the floor—difficult to work on, but for the same reason, not likely to be noticed. By the time Scott was assigned to food service, much of the sawing had been completed by relays of men standing atop a table (and scrambling down at the sound of a guard's footsteps).

To prepare for his escape, Scott removed an electrical cord from the buffing machine used to polish the basement floor and acquired several pairs of rubber surgical gloves from the hospital. His plan was to finish sawing through the bars, climb out the window, shinny up an outside drain pipe to the roof of the prison, cross the roof, then use the cord to lower himself to the ground out of sight of the guard towers. The gloves were to be inflated, tied at the ends, and used as flotation devices. With this plan in mind, Scott told Parker he was going to escape and invited him to go along.

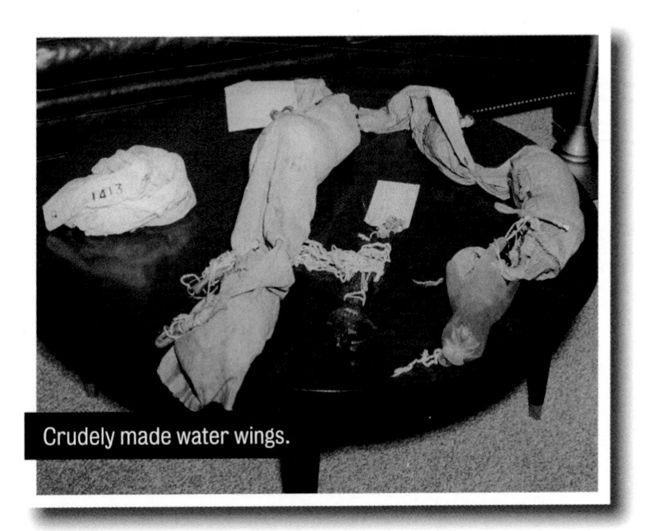
Crudely made water wings.

The Escape

On December 16, 1962, Scott and Parker were present for the 5:30 PM count. Immediately afterward, under the guise of taking garbage to the basement, Scott got in the elevator and took it down, then finished severing the bars. He then dashed to the elevator shaft and signaled for Parker, who jumped down the shaft. They broke the window with a crescent wrench that had been reported missing two years previous and fled through the opening. Quickly climbing two pipes at the corner of the building, they reached the roof, then sprinted across it to a blind spot and used the stolen cord to lower themselves directly behind the library. Under cover of fog and growing darkness, they scrambled down the steep hill on the western side of the island, then slid down the rugged cliffs by holding onto a sewage drain pipe; Parker broke his foot during the fall.

Once at the water's edge, they inflated the rubber gloves, inserted them into shirt sleeves and other pieces of material crudely stitched together, and tied the makeshift water wings around their waists. Barely fifteen minutes after they had last been counted, Scott ducked into the water and Parker followed. Scott

The escape window, seen from inside.

STATEMENT OF GUARD THOMAS J. LAMAR

On December 16, myself and Mr. Wentz were assigned to shake-down and pound bars in the kitchen basement. I went down to the basement at approximately 3:00 PM and I was there a half-hour to forty-five minutes; I left at about quarter to four. I specifically remember pounding the bars on the window that the inmates escaped through. I also visually inspected the bars on the window and noticed nothing out of the ordinary. Scott was present when we started inspecting the basement but he left shortly after we started. We completely checked all the bars along the side of the building.

We pounded the bars as we usually do, which is to pound them quite hard. They were pounded sufficiently to satisfy me that they were in good order.

claimed he saw lights on the mainland and began his frantic push toward them. The tide was swift—estimated at three knots—and the water temperature was about 46 degrees.

When the two were missed at 5:47 PM, the alarm was sounded and the search began. Thirty minutes later, officials found the broken window. Three forty-foot Coast Guard cutters, an eighty-two-foot patrol boat, and the Coast Guard's harbor tug criss-crossed the area between Alcatraz and the Golden Gate for the next hour and half.

The Aftermath

Parker, unable to break free of the current, took refuge on the outcrop of rocks known as Little Alcatraz, roughly one hundred yards from the prison island. At about 6:10 PM, prison guards picked him up, dripping wet and trembling from exposure. Scott half-swam, half-drifted in the choppy waters until he washed ashore on the rocks near Fort Point, at the southern base of the Golden Gate Bridge.

At 7:40, the Presidio's Military Police were told by telephone that teenagers had found a body at Fort Point. When the MPs and army fire department arrived at the scene, the "body" began to stir, and Scott—wearing only socks—was rushed to Letterman Hospital, nearly unconscious, with numerous cuts and scrapes; his clothes had been ripped from his body by the pounding surf. His body temperature had dropped to 94 degrees and he shook so convulsively that he couldn't speak. Doctors placed him in a thermo blanket, a rubber sleeping-bag–like device through which warm water circulated. Within thirty minutes, he was able to utter a few words, and by 10:45 that night, he was on his way back to Alcatraz. Scott and Parker were each given two-year sentences for escape, to run concurrently with their existing terms. Parker told the sentencing judge that he couldn't promise to refrain from future escape attempts.

BOP Director Bennett flew out from Washington to investigate the breakout. Expressing great confidence in the warden and staff, Bennett also said he would investigate why it took so long for word of the break to be sent to San Francisco police, who said they hadn't heard of it until one convict had already had reached the city's shore. In a letter to Bennett, Warden Blackwell wrote, "The fundamental weakness in our Alcatraz defenses is the antiquity of the institution, its inefficient layout, its many dark corners and the weaknesses that have developed over the years due to saltwater corrosion. . . . This escape is further evidence that Alcatraz has outlived its usefulness."

After the closing of Alcatraz, Scott was transferred to Leavenworth, then to Marion, Illinois, where he made another escape attempt. He died in 1987 in the Federal Correctional Institution in Tallahassee, Florida. Parker served time in Kansas and Georgia, where he was wounded in an attempt to climb over the prison wall. He too did a stint in Marion, from which he was paroled in 1974. He worked as a printer, and died in 1976.

Scott and Parker made front-page news in newspapers around the country. The *San Francisco Chronicle*'s "cold-water expert," George Lineer, said that Scott was "washed out toward the gate and if the eddy that caught him and tossed him on the rocks at Fort Point had been directed differently, Scott would have been on his way to Hawaii."

Reporters also questioned the fate of other Alcatraz escapees in light of Scott's amazing feat. It was twenty-five years to the day since the escape of Ted Cole and Ralph Roe—the first inmates to get off the island. And it was just six months after Frank Lee Morris and brothers John and Clarence Anglin fled into the bay. These five men made it into the water and were never found. Scott—a thirty-five-year-old university-educated bank robber—proved that a man could swim from Alcatraz and survive.

Fort Point, under the Golden Gate Bridge.

Go Get Them!

A Guard Recalls the Barker Escape

When Custodial Officer Ernest E. Padgett began his shift at midnight on January 13, 1939, he had no idea that within a few hours, he'd be taking part in a hunt for Doc Barker and his gang of would-be escapees (see Escape File 4). Officer Padgett came to Alcatraz in 1938 from the US Navy and spent four years on the island before signing up for the US Naval Reserve in 1942. A little more than two decades later, he wrote down his recollection of that early attempt.

Ernest Padgett, Alcatraz Island 1942.

My work that night began as it had any number of times in the past. There was almost no variation in the procedure, and I approached it in the matter-of-fact manner of any workman about to put in eight hours. I was assigned to the morning watch: 12 midnight to 8 AM.

At 11:45 PM, the lieutenant called the roll of all ongoing watch-standers in front of the main building, a concrete structure that sits atop the island. This building contains both the cellhouse—the prison proper—and the administrative offices. The lieutenant entered the cellhouse in company with the lieutenant of the outgoing watch for a count, and they emerged a few minutes later; there being about 250 inmates, the count went quickly and all was correct. The lieutenant posted his men and our shift took over.

My particular assignment was to patrol of the north half of the island—an outside (roving) patrol. Another man was assigned to the south part of the island, where most staff and families resided. Except for the lieutenant, we were the only men stationed outside and afoot. All other guards on duty were at various posts inside the cellhouse or stationed in the towers on either side of the island.

After accompanying some of the off-duty guards on the prison launch to and from San Francisco, I set out on the long stretch of my patrol. This took me from the dock area along a narrow beach on the east side of the island below the old army "sally port" and the staff's social hall to the power house and shop area on the north end. From there, I went through a set of double gates that led into the fenced-in shop area where for hours, I would divide my time between patrolling outside the buildings and searching the interior shops and prisoner lockers for contraband. Ordinarily, patrol wasn't boring. If the search became tiresome, it was always possible to stroll outside for some fresh air and a look at the scenery. Alcatraz—the hub of a scenic wheel—has an abundance of both.

On this particular shift, the scenery didn't last long. About 1:30 AM, the fog began to roll in. Soon, all outside lights except those a short distance away were obscured. The foghorn, only a few yards from where I was standing, commenced and kept up its rhythmic, nerve-grating blasts. All of this, of course, did nothing to add to my sense of well being, and I stuck pretty close to the shops, telephoning the armory every half hour as per standing instructions. As I went about my routine, the island's felons lay sleeping. At least, I thought they did.

Then the alarm sounded.

First a whistle, then the prison siren. Initially, their full meaning failed to register—*Must be a fire*, I thought. The idea of escape was slow to penetrate. Everyone had the utmost confidence in the tool-proof steel bars as well as the armed tower guards. (After this break, the BOP changed the term "tool proof" to "tool resistant.") Still not quite believing what I was hearing, I hurried to the nearest shop phone and called the armory. The voice at the other end of the line quickly set me straight: "Watch yourself. Five prisoners have broken out of isolation."

My sidearm was a .45 caliber army automatic, a good weapon for a single target at close range but inadequate for coping with five desperate men. I reasoned that although escaping prisoners are unpredictable, they would probably stay away from the fenced-in shop area and head for the unobstructed beaches on the opposite side of the island. As the situation wasn't covered by existing instructions, I decided to report to the cellhouse for emergency orders.

Gun in one hand and flashlight in the other, I made my way up the hill. The path was dimly lighted in some places and dark in others, and the swirling fog didn't help my anxiety. I expected the five to rush me from every rock and angle. The island abounds in rocks and angles.

By the time I got to the top of the hill and arrived at the front office, it was a very busy place. Firearms were being issued to all off-duty officers living on the island, and the deputy warden, standing near the front entrance, was giving a simply stated order: "They are out there somewhere. Go get them."

Any prison has a contingency plan for heading off escapees. Time and experience tell the staff which paths, which contours of land, which ravines an inmate will naturally follow in the dark while on the run. Alcatraz is a bit different. Its overall outline roughly resembles a battleship, with the main building, the prison, equivalent to a ship's superstructure. There are two other levels, a middle and lower. The middle has most of the employee housing on one side and the shops on the other. On the lower level is the dock. The rest is waterline. Though at many points, cliffs plunge directly into the water, approximately half of the island's perimeter is beach, which, depending on the tides, varies in width from almost nothing to ten or fifteen yards. Each level is connected with the other via a series of concrete ramps and stairways. From the cellhouse there is only one direction to go, and that's down to the water's edge.

Officers were armed and formed into groups of twos and threes. They fanned out down the hill and one by one, were enveloped by the foggy darkness. A manhunt at any time is not a pleasant business, but add the night, cotton-thick fog, and the moaning foghorns and the picture takes on an eerie quality. Ordinary shadows are distorted, even grotesque. Friend may look like foe, and with so many groups, each with its own arsenal, there was a grave danger of officers firing on one another.

After much bush-beating and probing, most of the groups neared the steep embankments on the second level overlooking the water's edge at various points around the island. I could hear commotion and shouting on the west side. There, aided by searchlights and a partial thinning of the fog, an officer on the cliff about forty feet above a small beach had spotted two escapees in the cove below.

Upon being hailed, the two men started running. They ignored the command to halt and increased their speed. Within seconds, they would have disappeared again into the fog and possibly the water. Officers carrying Thompson submachine guns opened fire and continued to fire until both figures were down. In the closeness of the fog, the shots were hardly recognizable as gunfire—the sound was more like hammers tapping on a wooden box.

Almost simultaneously with the shooting, two more escapees were discovered by other officers close by. The fifth and last was spotted within minutes in a cove a little farther up the beach. These three surrendered without a struggle. They were wet and shivering, and all, including the two wounded men, were naked or nearly so. The three non-casualties were ordered to climb back up the cliff's precipice. From there, they were herded into the cellhouse and then into cells. The two wounded men presented a problem. We had the choice of hauling them up a nearly perpendicular cliff with lines or picking them up by boat. Under the circumstances, the latter seemed to be a smoother operation.

The prison launch lowered a small skiff, which was taken into the cove and to the beach, where the wounded men were loaded on board; the skiff was then towed around the island to the dock on the east side. Under the glare of the dock lights, the two casualties were a messy sight. One had been shot on the right side of his forehead, and a pinkish froth oozed from the wound. The other had been hit in the legs and around the midriff. As he was transported from the boat to a stretcher, glistening rivulets of blood criss-crossed his bare skin in an odd pattern; it was as if someone had tossed a handful of bright red Christmas wrappings over his body. Both were alive. They were loaded onto a truck and taken to the prison hospital. The hunt was over.

Later investigation revealed that the five men had probably spent months sawing the bars of their cell fronts in the isolation block. Exact information was never obtained, and the "criminal brotherhood" is notoriously reticent about revealing trade secrets. On the beach, they found the waters of San Francisco Bay hostile toward their endeavor. They were probably facing an incoming tide, and, since they were on the west side of the island, it would have been like jumping into the wind, only to be blown back. Three were on the point of abandoning the attempt when discovered. All were considered "first line" felons, but only one had a claim to notoriety: Doc Barker, who had received the head wound.

It was about 5 AM and the excitement had now subsided. The off-duty officers returned to their quarters and I resumed patrol. As the fog gradually lifted, city lights were once again visible. The remainder of my watch was routine. Complete quiet prevailed, broken only by the murmur of waves slapping against rocks. The sky paled over the Berkeley-Oakland hills, then slowly, the top of Marin's Mount Tamalpais and the hills to the north turned pink. The purple hollows of the valleys around the bay gradually filled with light and the buildings of San Francisco came into view.

One by one, I turned off the lights of the shop area, then proceeded to the top to turn in my pistol to the armory. The day watch was taking over. Shortly after eight, I boarded the army steamer *General Coxe*, which picked up passengers at Alcatraz on its run from Angel Island to the Fort Mason docks in San Francisco. Fifteen minutes later, I was walking up Van Ness Avenue. Along the way, I stopped at a newsstand and picked up a paper. That's when I noticed the date: Friday the 13TH.

—This account was generously shared by
Officer Padgett's son, Wayne Padgett.